THE ITALIAN SEMINARS

D1563017

Wilfred R. Bion
THE ITALIAN SEMINARS

Translated by
Philip Slotkin

KARNAC
LONDON   NEW YORK

First published in 2005 by
H. Karnac (Books) Ltd.
6 Pembroke Buildings, London NW10 6RE

Copyright © 2005 The Estate of Wilfred R. Bion

Earlier edition published in Italian by Edizioni Borla in 1985, *Seminari italiani: Testo completo dei Seminari tenuti da W. R. Bion a Roma.*

The rights of Wilfred R. Bion to be identified as the author of this work have been asserted in accordance with §§ 77 and 78 of the Copyright Design and Patents Act 1988.

All rights reserved. No part of this publication may be reproduced, stored in a retrieval system, or transmitted, in any form or by any means, electronic, mechanical, photocopying, recording, or otherwise, without the prior written permission of the publisher.

British Library Cataloguing in Publication Data

A C.I.P. for this book is available from the British Library

 ISBN: 978-1-85575-339-6

10 9 8 7 6 5 4 3 2 1

Edited, designed, and produced by Communication Crafts

www.karnacbooks.com

CONTENTS

EDITORIAL NOTE

The seminars contained in this volume were held by Bion in Rome in the summer of 1977. Parthenope Bion Talamo translated/interpreted at all the seminars—both Bion's English into Italian and the questions and comments from the Italian participants into English for Bion. It was an exceptional *tour de force* on her part. I subsequently edited Bion's contributions for the Italian edition of the seminars, which was published in 1985.

Francesca Bion, 2005

NOTE FROM THE ITALIAN EDITION

The complete text of these seminars, held by Bion in Rome in 1977, has never previously been published in book form, not even in English. The seminars were carried out in two series: the first, consisting of four sessions, was held under the auspices of the Società Italiana Psicoanalitica; the second, of five sessions, was organized by the Via Pollaiolo Research Group.

Parthenope Bion Talamo, 1985

THE ITALIAN SEMINARS

Rome, 8 July 1977

First, I must apologize for not being able to speak Italian, but I am consoled by the thought that the subject I want to discuss is one which I find very difficult to talk about in *any* language, even when I am able to mobilize all the English that I know. I shall have reason to revert to this point later.

What are we concerned with? What are we all here for? What are we going to talk about? Of course, we could say "psychoanalysis", but the word simply doesn't mean anything. It is a term which is used if we want to "talk about it", but it doesn't say what "it" is. You can't smell it, you can't touch it, you can't see it, and indeed it is very difficult to say what the sensible component of psychoanalysis is.

In so far as we claim to have a scientific outlook, it is usually supposed that there must be some supporting evidence. What I would like to touch on here is how important it is to have a foundation of fact, and how those facts should be observed by us.

My training in the British Institute of Psycho-Analysis, my experience with John Rickman, with Melanie Klein—all of it was verbal. Are we supposed to be blind and deaf to everything except what comes in through the ears? When a patient comes to see me, there is, in fact, a body which I can see for myself, and to that extent I can fall back on the evidence of my senses and on the information which my senses bring me. I don't think that we can afford to ignore what our senses tell us, because the facts are very few anyway.

So far the most valuable thing I have is the evidence of my senses and the information that my senses bring me. When I say "senses", I am borrowing a term from anatomy and physiology and using it as a model in order to be able to talk about other things for which I haven't the same sort of evidence. In this respect I am dependent upon having a healthy nervous system which can be irritated—using the term in a physiological sense: our nerve endings are irritated by the universe in which we are living. Some of those senses are extremely powerful. For example, the sense of sight and ocular capacity appears to achieve a dominant role largely because I can see things even when I can't touch them. To some extent the same thing can be said about hearing: I can hear without having actual physical contact with a physical body.

I would like to draw attention to a quotation from Freud's paper of 1926: "There is much more continuity between intra-uterine life and earliest infancy than the impressive caesura of the act of birth allows us to believe" (*S.E.* 20, p. 138). He had expressed it before, but he never seemed to follow it through; it came too near the end of his life. Also unfortunately—partly, I think, because of an intervention by Ernest Jones, who seems to me to have prejudiced Freud against Otto Rank—Rank wasn't really able to carry his ideas about the trauma of birth very far. He built up the trauma of birth: Freud tended to ignore the fact of that "impressive caesura". But Freud, being what he was, still appreciated that there was a truth in the fact of birth and the fact that it was a very impressive event.

I want to suggest that we should take the hint and make allowances for the fact that we are unduly impressed by the trauma of birth. I do it this way: When were you born? What was your birthplace? If you gave me the ordinarily accepted answers, I could say, "No, that is very useful for the vital statistics of the government who wants to know your birthday was on such-and-such a day of such-and-such a month of such-and-such a year. That would suit them fine." But I would like to be able to say, "Please tell me when your optic pits, at about the third somite, became functional. Tell me when your auditory pits became functional." Of course, I know perfectly well that nobody can answer that question.

I could ask a number of questions—I wouldn't expect you to try to answer them; I wouldn't try to answer them myself. Nevertheless, without a scrap of supporting evidence, I believe that they are relevant questions.

The embryologists tell us that there is evidence of the survival in the human body of what they call "branchial clefts". It is an interesting idea, and one could play around with it. But that would be more suitable if we had been—or were, or still had elements surviving in our make-up which would be appropriate to our being—fishes. The embryologists also talk about vestigial tails. If these vestiges exist with regard to the body, why couldn't they be hanging around somewhere even with regard to what we call our minds? Is it possible that some of our characteristics would be more comprehensible if we were water-living animals? Or if we lived in trees like monkeys? It is not very difficult to see why people often talk—somewhat metaphorically—about our simian ancestors and our simian characteristics; not so often with regard to our fishy ones—although surgeons do talk about a "branchial cleft tumour". Although they are not operating on the embryo, they make use of what the embryologists tell us to carry out a surgical operation of a sophisticated kind on what they still call a "branchial cleft tumour".

What I want to draw attention to is this idea that the human animal has a mind, or a character, or a personality. It seems to be quite a useful theory, and we behave as if we thought it was more than that. When it comes to being psychoanalysts and psychiatrists, this cannot be treated as if it were simply an entertaining theory. Nor do patients come to see us because they are suffering from an entertaining theory. We could say that there is one collaborator we have in analysis on whom we can rely, because he behaves as if he really had a mind and because he thought that somebody not himself could help. In short, the most important assistance that a psychoanalyst is ever likely to get is not from his analyst, or supervisor, or teacher, or the books that he can read, but from his patient. The patient—and only the patient—knows what it feels like to be him or her. The patient is also the only person who knows what it feels like to have ideas such as that particular man or woman has. That is why it is so important that we should be able to hear, see, smell, even feel what information the patient is trying to convey. He is the only one who knows the facts; therefore, those facts are going to be the main source of any interpretation, any observation, which we are likely to be able to make. Our first consideration therefore has to be, how are we to observe if we take that scientific view of the importance of evidence—the evidence which is available to us for that very short space of time, fifty minutes or whatever it is, for which the patient agrees to make himself available? It is very important that every single one of us should decide for himself what is his minimum requirement in order to be able to do analysis.

It appears to me that the evidence which is available to my senses directly is worth incomparably more than the evidence which can be brought to me through "hearsay". To imagine a value, for the sake of this discussion, I could say that the evidence which is available when the patient is with me is 99%; what I hear said about the patient or my conduct of the case, or anything else, is worth 1% at most. So from that point of view, whatever I hear said or reported as soon as the patient has left my sight and hearing, I don't need to bother about very much; I can be deaf and blind to anything else. It saves a lot of trouble, I admit, but I think it also has a lot of sense behind it.

We now come back again to the questions, what are we observing, and what are we to do about our observations? I remember being asked, "Do you ever do anything besides talk?" I said, "Yes, I am silent." I'm afraid it may be difficult for you to believe when I sit here and talk, but in fact in analysis I like to be able to remain silent. It is, as we know, very difficult, because pressure is put on us to say or *do* something. "Why don't you *say* something?" "Why don't you *do* something?" This is particularly the case when one is dealing with a patient who is dependent—a child, say—on parents or relatives who want the analyst to do something. By that they mean do something which they can understand. It is difficult for lay people to believe that we employ a kind of talking which is indistinguishable from action.

We become so careless about our vocabulary in ordinary social contact that the words we use, the language we talk, becomes debased, devalued. I think it is therefore very important to get as clear as you can *your* language, the language which *you* use both for communication with yourself and for communication with somebody who is not you.

In your introspection I don't think it is a good thing to concentrate on writing what you think the patient has said—a sort of case history. That kind of narrative can be useful; I don't want to dismiss it, and perhaps we shall talk about it further later. But, in the meantime, think of what words you most often use in analysis, cut them down to fewer and fewer, and then use them very sparingly, very exactly, only in order to say what you mean. If you use very few words, and if you always use them correctly—meaning relating directly to what you think or feel yourself—then the patient may gradually understand the language which is spoken by you. Patients will often say to me, "I don't understand what you mean." There are two possible answers to that: one is that there is no particular reason why they should, because they are not familiar with the matters I am talking about; the other is that they don't understand my use of those few words which I use. But it is very difficult indeed for patients to believe that I say what I mean. In a way they are quite right—very few people say what they mean. So it is hard to believe that that is what the analyst is doing. In time they may discover, extraordinary though it is, that the analyst is meaning what he says, or at least is trying to say what he means, which is very difficult. It is like doing a surgical operation and having to sharpen your scalpels and get them into working order *while* you are operating. So, while you are practising analysis, you have also to practise sharpening and making precise the vocabulary which you use. It is important to be sure what your vocabulary is, those few words which are really useful to you, and to keep them up to date and in a condition in which they can convey your meaning.

To digress for a moment: Why talk? It is a very recently acquired skill. I suppose the human animal has invented and developed articulate speech only in the last few thousand years—no time at all. So there is a great deal to be said for verbal communication and for keeping it as near to accuracy as we can get it. However, I don't think it is a good thing to ignore the fact that there are other forms of communication. Even verbal communication has been made by carving letters in stone. There are others who carve and sculpt shapes which are also methods of communication. Recently people like Henry Moore and Barbara Hepworth have carved shapes with holes in them. That is a resort to a method of communication in which there also has to be a receiver; it assumes that somebody will look at the sculpture. Similarly, painters use pigments—like the Impressionists. The Impressionist painters—and indeed all painters—are falling back on the communication of light; they can use varieties of colours, different ranges of the visual spectrum. It would be useful if you could consider for yourselves the various methods of communication that are known to you, their respective merits, and the extent to which they are capable of great subtlety.

I have talked for a long time, and I personally find it very difficult to tolerate information about questions I have not asked. Therefore, I think it would be a good thing if you could state what the questions are that you *do* want to ask, and then between the lot of us perhaps we could find some kind of response.

Q: If you like, I can start, just to break the ice. Compliments and the like aside, neither I nor the rest of the group was prepared for Dr Bion's subject matter, but, of course, I was very impressed by the element of surprise, the form of expression and the pathos conveyed throughout. At the same time, I was quite surprised to discover that it fitted in with one of my own professional interests at this time—namely, the symbolic function of emotions. What I mean is the function of emotions as signs—that particular warhorse of late Freud—or a whole series of concepts used by Hartmann and other psychologists of his school, which have recently been taken up again by Rangell. I'm referring to the function of emotions as signs: emotions that perform an information function in themselves. Of course, it isn't the information function that sums up the content and meaning of emotions, although it certainly represents a good part of them. So when you talked about using the sense of smell, and all the senses, it seemed to me that you were somehow also referring to the possibility of nonverbal communication—that is, all the emotional forms we use to communicate both with ourselves (because they are intrapsychic symbols) and also, in a way, for communicating with others. Although they need not necessarily be translated into words, they also supply the patient with a reinterpretation of his phantasy or of the object of his perceptions. So I'd like to ask you now whether you would also include emotions among these non-linguistic forms of communication.

BION: I think that what the patient feels is the nearest thing to a fact—as I ordinarily understand it—that he is ever likely to experience. The same thing applies to myself. For example, an infant seems to be "aware"—the best word I can use—of its "dependence". Inseparable from this, it also seems to be aware of being "all alone". I think both feelings are unpleasant, and I think they are both fundamental. An infant also seems to be aware that there is what we should call a personality present which it could depend upon; at the same time, that infant can be aware that there is not another person there.

With regard to patients who are described as being "psychotic" or "borderline psychotic", I think they are extremely aware of things which most of us have learnt not to be aware of.

Let us take that same infant twenty, thirty, forty, fifty years later. You, as the analyst, are getting a bit tired, so you fall back on theories, theories which I think are difficult to differentiate from what Freud calls "paramnesias", which are intended to fill this space which is left because somebody has forgotten some particular point and therefore invents something to fill that space. In that way one could argue that the whole of psychoanalysis is a kind of beautiful paramnesia worked out, made consistent with itself, a sort of architectonic in which every bit is in its proper place—only, here and there there seem to be things which are paradoxes which start to emerge. When we are tired, our remarkably cosmetic conversation, which sounds exactly like psychoanalysis, in fact becomes jargon. In short, it is like the well-known statement that people try to make deep noises from the chest sound like profound thoughts. When this happens, the borderline psychotic will react in a way which shows that he knows that the analyst who was there has now become absent in mind.

I don't know if that is what you have been talking about, but it seems to me that it is very similar—this extraordinary communication. It is not physical, as far as we know, and yet an emotion is communicated from one body to the other—or, I suppose one ought to say, from one mind to the other.

Q: If possible, I'd like to take another look at the problem that was touched on at the beginning and go into it in greater depth— that is, the problem of the trauma of birth and the subsequent comments about the animal vestiges in human beings. After all, it seems to me that in what Dr Bion has said there is a kind of transition from the actual trauma of birth to what we might call the concept of a birthday: being born is one thing, but remembering one's birthday is another—that is, the moment when one began to feel, to see and to laugh. So I was very excited by this fact—whether the problem can be seen, to use Dr Bion's language, from this vertex. Dr Bion's emphasis on the need for the analyst to specify his own language to himself extremely precisely basically means, it seems to me, that the analyst must be absolutely sure that he is saying what he is really feeling. So when the analyst feels, more or less, that he is really saying what he is thinking and feeling, and therefore is genuinely becoming conscious of what is going on inside him, can this moment be compared with the transition from feeling to articulate language that you mentioned earlier in the seminar? If this corresponds to the aspect of birth as a birthday—that is, not of birth in the sense of when one comes into the world, but of birth as the time when one becomes conscious of one's own perceptions and of what one feels—then the real question is this: might this process of self-specification and, as we might say, self-assumption of his own language by the analyst really be the analyst's repeated trauma of birth in analysis, and might the patient be in the position of a spectator of this ongoing process of birth of the analyst? And finally, how can the birth of the analyst be linked up with the birth of the patient? What is involved in terms of identification, learning, nonverbal communication, and so on?

BION: It would take me a very long time even to start answering the number of questions you have posed. But I would like to draw attention to a passage in Tolstoy's *War and Peace* in which Prince

Andrei says, "That is sooth; accept it"; that is a feeling he has, and he communicates that feeling very clearly in those words. I don't know what validity is to be attached to it, but I do know that there are certain situations in the consulting-room in which *both* people are illuminated.

Translating the same thing into slightly different language: two people have a sexual relationship; they say—they can even get a licence for it—that they are married. Sometimes both of them have an experience about which they feel, "That is really an expression of love." In that way the two of them learn what passionate love is in an unmistakable manner, and measured against that experience you can re-assess all the other kinds of sexual relationships you have had—even with the same partner—and what a difference there is between them. Whether it is possible ever to bend this recently acquired capacity for verbal communication so that it could approximate to a description of passionate love is another matter. When you consider the cultural history of the human race, how many poets, philosophers, saints do you think have ever approximated to describing that extraordinary experience of passionate love? In fact, the words, the vocabulary, is so debased—so that many people have learnt how to talk about "love", "hate" and so forth—that it is a commonplace for people to say, "Yes, I know; yes, I know; yes, I know." They really think they do, but they don't know the first thing about it. It is possible to say, "Of course I know 'Les Coquelicots'—I've seen countless reproductions of it." Or, "Yes, I know Mozart's Horn Concerto—I've heard lots and lots of recordings of it." But they haven't experienced the "real thing".

After the last rehearsal of *Petrouchka*, the producer said, "No, it's not right." Both Fokine and Stravinsky were staggered by this idea that it wasn't right—it ended, if you remember, with the death of Petrouchka. When Fokine and Stravinsky attacked him and said, "Well, how ought it to end?" he said, "The ghost of Petrouchka must appear." So, although that was supposed to be the final rehearsal, they set to work again and changed the end so that the ghost of Petrouchka appeared on the wall, fantastically waving its arms.

What is that object which purports to be the ghost of an inanimate doll and which one would think had been dead all the time, having simply made gestures as if animated, pulled by the puppet-master's strings? Putting it another way: when you see your patient tomorrow, will you be able to detect, in the material which is available to you, signs that there is a ghost of a puppet? If you can, you may still be able to breath some life into that tiny survival.

Q: I'd like to ask Dr Bion something. I have detected two smells in everything you have said here. The first was the smell of the things you said, which seems to me to be a smell of facts, and then there was another smell—in my view, a smell of theories. I'd like to know your personal impression of this and whether these two things are inevitably always mixed up with each other.

Bion: It depends what you mean by "inevitably". I think splitting has a very long history. For example, the diaphragm, separating the upper part of the anatomy from the lower part, was quite sensibly seen as the location of the spirit or soul because it goes up and down as one breathes; it's perfectly obvious that that is what makes people think or get frightened. So much for the anatomical facts, and so much for the ideas. It is quite rational, it is based on good observation, and it becomes an impenetrable theory until somebody penetrates it. According to Democritus of Abdera, the useless mass of the brain has something to do with thinking. You can see for yourself what a silly idea that is: it doesn't *do* anything. So a theory that the brain has anything to do with thinking is really fantastic and is unsupported by any evidence. Well—not quite, because some genius discovers that if you tackle this brain matter, in spite of its bony covering, with, for example, a battle-axe, that will put an end to troublesome thinking. So there could grow up the idea that that drastic and violent form of operation reveals the source or origin of thought.

We have become so intelligent that I have heard it said that ideas don't exist in infants and embryos because the fibres aren't myelinated—therefore they cannot possibly think. But I have seen a very young baby who was frightened; I have seen a baby put on the pot and immediately "do its stuff". Does its bottom think? Or has it no myelinated fibres and therefore cannot? Or shall we have to reconsider our physiological knowledge?

The same thing applies to the whole body of psychoanalytic thinking. These theories are very useful—the difference between the conscious and the unconscious. Falling back on metaphor, one could say that when we secrete an idea, or when we produce a theory, we seem at the same time to lay down chalky material, we become calcified, the idea becomes calcified, and then you have another impressive caesura which you can't break out of. An asset, a useful theory of conscious and unconscious, then becomes a liability; it becomes a caesura which we cannot penetrate.

Dr Matte Blanco has spoken quite a lot about the possibility of thoughts or ideas which have never been conscious. I would certainly agree from an analytic point of view, from my experience of analysis, that there are certain ideas which appear never to have been conscious and which even seem to betray their existence in adult life. For example, I have a patient who talks very freely, and at the end of a session I know a great deal—if I were to attach much importance to hearsay evidence—about everybody except the patient. That seems to me to become a bit more comprehensible if one supposes that this patient has tried to get rid of every undesirable thought, feeling, even primordial thought, before he ever had them, so that he is surrounded, so to speak, by the thoughts which are voiced by other people—according to the patient—but never his own thoughts or ideas—never: he hasn't any; they have all been evacuated. One wonders if it is possible to mobilize what could be described as a mathematical capacity, or mathematical thinking, to express that state of affairs in a way that would be communicable to other people. Using as much analytic theory as seemed relevant, I made no difference whatsoever to this flow of material in which everything appeared excepting the patient—the one object which was completely unexpressed. I have given plenty of interpretations about projection and so on and so forth; they make no difference. There is something about the total evacuation which requires some different form of approach.

A patient tells me that he has had a dream and that he dreamt . . . whatever it is. That is a narrative account. It could be described, borrowing from mathematics, as a linear progression from A to B. The individual is born, marries, dies. *Hic iacet.* There's the whole story—finished. But a problem arises when you want to draw the patient's attention to something which requires a more subtle delineation than a linear progression from birth to death.

Patients will very freely confess sins—lots of them—and after a time one feels that there is an inexhaustible supply of mistakes, crimes, failures with which to keep the analysis going. But if an analysis is turned into a somewhat elaborate version of the confessional known to the Church, it will not do. So even restricting ourselves to articulate speech, it is important to be able to decide when an analysis has turned into a kind of modern version of the confessional. If it has, then we may miss drawing attention to what the patient has got right.

I have experienced this curious state of affairs in which it would seem that the Freudian architectonic requires readjustment, particularly in the direction of leaving room for growth. While we are trying to elaborate a system of thought, or a system of analysis, we have to be aware that we are also excreting a kind of calcification which is going to make those thoughts become more of a prison than a liberating force.

Melanie Klein was rather annoyed at being labelled a "Kleinian"; she considered that she was an ordinary psychoanalyst and was simply following on the established theories of psychoanalysis. Betty Joseph said, "It's too late. Whether you like it or not you are a Kleinian"; she couldn't escape from that. And then, under the pressure of the various objections to her brainchild, she became more and more dogmatic and, I think, further and further from being able to draw attention to the merits of certain ideas which deserve to be given a chance to grow and develop.

This matters to us tomorrow when we see our patient. I think it is helpful to forget all our theories and our desires because they are so obstructive that they become an impressive caesura which we cannot get past. The problem is how to let the germ of an idea, or the germ of an interpretation, have a chance of developing.

If I want to pictorialize this, I can talk about alpha- and beta-elements—a beta-element being something which is purely physical; an alpha-element something mental, like the idea that a baby is able to think if it knows what to do when a pot is put under its bottom. Take the next stage of the development, when it becomes something you can very nearly pictorialize: I would like to say, "Where did you go last night, and what did you see?" I am not really very interested in the fact that you went to bed and went to sleep. I would still like to know where you went and what you saw. Under pressure you might admit, "Oh well, I had a dream—but I don't remember it." Freud regarded the interpretation of dreams as being very important—it is hardly surprising when you consider how very early in history certain dreams have been recorded, such as those which appear in the Bible. However, while I agree, I think it is also liable to become—has, indeed, already become—a structure which is very difficult to break out of. When the patient says he "dreamt" something, we think—rightly or wrongly—that he was asleep. The places that he went to and the things that he saw were visited, and seen in, a certain frame of mind. When he is wide awake and conscious he is in a different state of mind, and the story that he saw such-and-such is sure to be falsified because it is told when he is fully conscious. The experience was had when he was in a quite different frame of mind—"asleep" or "unconscious".

To come back to tomorrow's session: what you have to do is to give the germ of a thought a chance. You are sure to object to it; you are sure to wish it conformed to some cherished psychoanalytic theory, so that if you said it to some other psychoanalyst it could be seen to be in accordance with psychoanalytic theory, or the theories of your supervisor or your analyst. That is not good enough for what you tell *yourself*. Therefore—and this is really the central point, but very difficult—you have to *dare* to think and feel whatever it is that you think or feel, no matter what your society or your Society thinks about it, or even what *you* think about it. I can try to classify these thoughts and feelings as speculative imaginations, speculative ideas and speculative reasons. But I don't think that we should therefore allow ourselves to be misled into supposing that these speculative thoughts have the same status as that which scientists ascribe to facts. As far as facts are concerned, I would think that they add up to evidence supporting a particular belief, idea or theory. The things I am talking about do not amount to anything better than a probability—something for which there is inadequate or insufficient supporting evidence. Even a person with as acute a mind as J. M. Keynes wrote on the Theory of Probability. But I am very doubtful that that kind of mathematics is good enough to further the problem of probability; there is something about the precision of mathematics which is valuable, but at the same time that precision must not be allowed to become so ossi-fied, so calcified, that there is no room for development.

More recently, Brower and Heyting have attempted to release mathematics from the prison of present mathematical thinking by the elaboration of Intuitionism. Gödel has done the same thing with regard to meta-mathematics, which has involved questioning the law of the excluded middle.

I would like to be on the side of any of these things which have been excluded, whether it is the diaphragm which separates the top from the bottom, or whatever it is. Later I shall hope to talk about the excluded part of psychoanalysis, or what will be ex-cluded from your consulting-room tomorrow when you and your analysand meet. The excluded part plays a large part and may not even yet have emerged into psychoanalytic theory.

Rome, 9 July 1977

Q : Before yesterday's seminar, I was curious to know what Dr Bion thought about music. I'd been reflecting on an analytic experience of mine when I felt that a woman patient preferred music to analysis and was trying— and had begun—to find music in analysis too, for certain reasons: music banished visual experiences, especially terrifying ones associated with the phobic space. She was able to dissolve the terrifying experiences of sounds by putting them together in a melody and using only certain sounds or certain limited pitches. If the music was broken down, the sounds took on a terrifying quality reminiscent of the terror of the visual, almost bodily, three-dimensional images of a claustrophobic space. But I had attributed this possibility of seeing terrifying images to her phantasy of a Cyclopean eye—the third mental eye that psychologists talk about—which she seems to see graphically before her.

An experience with another analysand puts me in mind of Ulysses, who turned himself into "Nobody" so as not to be seen and eaten by Polyphemus. So I wondered if Dr Bion feels we can also invoke a Cyclopean perception that has to do with music and analysis, as some psychologists have demonstrated.

Does Dr Bion think there is any connection between all this and the problem of musicians who play without reading the notes and others who can only play if they have a score in front of them?

BION: If your patient is a musician or has musical capacity, then it is likely that in the consulting-room you can hear words *and* music. The patient's problem is not simply his relationship with the analyst. Obviously the analyst is a person the patient only meets for a few sessions a week for a limited period—it is not supposed to be a permanent attachment. Then why does the patient come at all? It certainly cannot be because he disagrees with the analyst, or likes the analyst, for the analyst is not a person of any importance. As far as we are concerned, the real trouble is the patient's dis-agreement with himself. The psychoanalytic theory that there are mental conflicts is easily lost sight of but is, in fact, very important. However, as a temporary affair, what you can see is something of the relationship between those two people—the analyst and the analysand.

Falling back on the report of what happened—and this is what makes this kind of discussion of it of secondary importance—what would happen to you if you were bombarded with words as this patient bombards his analyst? Suppose the analyst is sensitive to what he is seeing and being told by the patient—that is what we are theoretically supposed to be. Taking first of all the words: what—as far as the analyst is concerned—are the nerve endings which are being stimulated? There is a wide range of stimulation of the analyst: the remnants of his classical education, knowledge of Greek mythology, knowledge or experience of any other culture. He is now free to show who he is by picking on, say, Greek mythology, or psychoanalytical theory or psychological theory. So from this point of view the analyst is invited to express his opinion of who he is.

What about the musical accompaniment of this mass of verbal information and stimulation? The patient is really giving a performance of a full operatic experience, of words and music. The problem is, what is the analyst to do? Whatever he does, the patient will have something to go on, something the patient can then himself interpret.

Again identifying oneself with the analyst: what are you to do when you are bombarded with such a vast variety of mythology, story, classical history and music? There is the further point that the analysand probably knows that the analyst is medically qualified; he can therefore always stimulate or not, as he chooses, the medical knowledge of the analyst. For example, this particular patient might show bodily symptoms of a blood disease. What is the analyst to do when he feels that the patient needs medical treatment and, at the same time, the analyst wants to be an analyst? I pose the question because those in a sufficiently hostile community will be very glad to bring accusations of malpractice against the doctor who has failed to interpret that the trouble was not mental at all, but that the patient had this, that or the other blood disease. I have known this happen: the analyst was accused of having failed to diagnose that it was a case of cancer and of having gone on—according to the patient—mistakenly interpreting in psychoanalytical terms a cancerous condition which finally destroyed the patient.

I should be suspicious about so much "noise" made by a patient who bombarded me with such a mass of facts. The analyst can be deafened, blinded and put in the position where he virtually cannot use his senses because they are *all* being bombarded.

Suppose the patient shows signs of physical disease but just passes it off. I think in that instance I would say, "With regard to the physical complaint you have made, you will, of course, be seeing your doctor. But *here* we must consider something else." Out of all this variety of material from which I am invited to choose, I would like to select what appears to me to be psychoanalytically relevant. That is quite simple as a general theory; in practice, it is not. In such a mass of information the noise is so great that you cannot hear the noise you ought to be hearing. The impression that it creates on me is that if I were subjected to that experience, my attention would be drawn to the repetition of this word "terrible"—it kept cropping up. I would strongly suspect that this is the vestigial remains of something that I would regard as sub-thalamic fear. I am not using that phrase as an expression of my medical or psychoanalytical or any other knowledge. As far as I am concerned it is an idea which belongs to what I have described as "speculative imagination".

Now that is all very well for me: it is not good enough for me to transform my impressions into a psychoanalytical theory, or a psychoanalytical interpretation. Therefore, I would want to hear more, and the minimum condition for me to analyse that patient is to be allowed to remain silent, because I don't want to add my noise to that which the patient is already making. *If* I am allowed more time to be silent, then I may be able to hear just a little bit more.

The situation in analysis is misleading because there is apparently only one person there with the analyst. I have found my experiences in groups useful—a group is almost like one person, character or personality, spread out over a space. In a group I would want to know, "Who is this person who is saying, 'terrified . . . terrified . . . terrible'?" Similarly, if I were a physician I would want to see the whole body, and then perhaps I could locate a swelling, or a flush of the skin, and I could wonder, "Is this some sort of infection?" As I say, in the group one could then locate, so to speak, the origin, the source, of the infection.

Having taken that sort of group view, narrow down your observation. At this point I would be paying much more attention to this "terrible" and listening to the occurrence, apparently, only of a word; but I would hope, if I am given a chance of remaining silent, to be able to detect a certain similarity about all these "terribles". And then when I thought that things had gone far enough for me to feel that I could formulate my observation, I would do so. But I would ignore all the rest of it.

However, there is still this point that included in this is also the music. The two of them together would perhaps make it a bit easier to see or recognize the centre of infection, the point which really requires to be interpreted. That is much more difficult than it sounds in a discussion like this. The experience of practical analysis or practical medicine, or the practice of anything, is very much tougher than the discussion about it.

Q: Someone told me about a psychiatric institution where, over a period, a professor gave identical red sweaters to a number of mothers, who held their babies in their arms until, after a while, the sweaters were taken back and placed together on a carpet. Then all the babies were put down beside the sweaters, all of which were the same colour, and quite a few were able to find their mother's sweater, presumably by the smell. But then, the head of the institute where I worked for many years boasted that he could identify a person's schizophrenic state from the particular smell he or she gave off while in that state. I had never experienced this and doubted that it was true, until one day I was analysing a schizoid, perverse patient, who had great difficulty in expressing some of his feelings in words: it turned out that in some sessions he was putting out a very particular smell, which tended to put me in a dream-like state in which quite disturbing images came up in my mind. I mention this because it seems to me that we have had a lot to say about nonverbal communication here.

BION: The nonverbal communication is very difficult to interpret, to transform or translate into articulate speech. That applies both to the analyst and to the analysand. The analysand likewise expects that he will have to talk an articulate language with his analyst, and he hasn't any words with which to do it. This happens in a variety of different ways—here, we can discuss it again, not only with regard to this particular patient, but to recognize a certain similarity between that kind of communication and the patient who responds with floods of tears. Tears, like smiles, don't mean a thing. So the analysand is up against this problem of finding a method of communicating what he wants to say. Falling back on a narrative view of the situation—from birth to death—smell can be one of the long-range methods of communication. Therefore, some stage in the development of the patient—or, as I would put it, some aspect of this patient at the present moment—still betrays a survival of that state, or what I am compelled to call "a state of mind". Where is this smell located? Anatomically and physiologically we can produce all sorts of theories based on our knowledge of embryology and so forth, but, ignoring that for the moment, where is it cropping up with these apparently two people in the room? I say "apparently two people" because of the dominance of what one could call a rational point of view—there are only two anatomical structures in the room. But it is difficult to know how many minds or personalities there are there, and which one is the source of that smell.

Again indulging in speculative imagination, I would say that this patient finds it very difficult indeed to say that he is coming for mental nourishment. If he could by any chance re-mobilize extremely primitive equipment, then perhaps he could smell the place where he expects to find mental nourishment. But suppose that, at the same time, the patient is afraid of making a smell which would make *him* locatable so that something could come and prey on him. In that way I would begin to suspect that he is sometimes afraid that he will get devoured, and sometimes afraid that the analyst will notice that *he* is being fed upon, being used to provide mental nourishment.

Then why not say so? Why not say that he wants an analysis, that he wants to have his emotional or intellectual needs satisfied? The obvious answer would be, "Because he can't." Articulate speech, which can be comprehended by somebody else and which the patient can understand, is not available to him. So he is afraid that there is no chance of getting the help he wants from the analyst. This is a very common state indeed. I still find it astonishing how few patients believe that any relief can be obtained. And the same thing applies to analysts: they do not feel that they have any evidence that the kind of conversation that takes place in analysis will satisfy anybody or anything. It takes a long time before it becomes clear that, in fact, the analytic intercourse is yielding an experience which is nourishing to both parties.

The same thing applies to the patient who repeats "terrible, terrible". All that is said in a vague hope that somebody or something will turn up who will be able to understand what he is communicating and will be able to supply the correct mental nourishment. It is a matter of touch and go whether the patient will be able to come to analysis long enough to find out if it is worth doing.

The kind of thing I have been saying is something of a generalization. From day to day, from free-association to free association, one is dealing with a little bit of that fundamental story. In the one instance there is this problem of how to find something to feed on without getting eaten up in the process; in the other, how to let anybody know that he is terrified, especially in a situation where there may be nobody. In this way both patients resort to a some-what obscure, primitive and incomprehensible method of communication. Then they can feel, "Well, nothing comes of it, but it doesn't matter. It's not worse than it was before." But if the analyst has been able to give enough interpretations to lead the patient to think there could be somebody who understands, then terror is released.

To make that point clearer, using a pictorial image: a party of some five people were survivors from a shipwreck. The rest had died of starvation or had been swept overboard from the remnants of the raft. They experienced no fear whatsoever—but became terrified when they thought a ship was coming near. The possibility of rescue, and the even greater possibility that their presence would not be noticed on the surface of the ocean, led them to be terrified. Previously the terror had been sunk, so to speak, in the overwhelming depths of depression and despair.

So the analyst, in the midst of the noises of distress, the failure of analysis, the uselessness of that kind of conversation, still needs to be able to hear the sound of this terror which indicates the position of a person beginning to hope that he might be rescued.

Consider this patient who smells the possibility that the analyst could nourish him, but also that the analyst might devour him. Let us put that into more rational terms: will the analyst understand him? Or will the analyst shut him up in a mental hospital so he will never escape? What interpretation do you give? This highly sophisticated one, saying, "You are afraid of getting locked up in a mental hospital"?—in which case he might not understand why the analyst is talking like that or what it has to do with what he is saying. That question can only be decided by the analyst or analysand, or both of them, because it is such an extremely subtle position. That is why I don't like butting in with theories which are out of touch with the actual patient and the actual experience. I would again say that the more the analyst appreciates the extremely wealthy circumstance of an actual session to which the patient comes, the greater chance he may have of being able to make up his mind: "No, I won't give that interpretation, I'll give this one."

If I say he is afraid of getting locked up in a mental hospital, it may frighten this terrified patient so much that he cannot go on with the analysis. Or if I say he has no sense of smell, the situation would again be hopeless. It is necessary to give an interpretation which lets the patient have a chance of knowing that he has been understood, and a chance of feeling that he will not be incarcerated or devoured.

This is partly a by-product of the fact that, thanks to articulate speech, we do seem to establish a contact, a verbal intercourse. Therefore, the patient who has these terrifying experiences can be afraid that the terror will be communicated to the analyst, and if he, the patient, doesn't run away, the analyst will. Falling back on the group experience, I can say that the patient is afraid of a situation which can develop into fight or flight and can express itself on sophisticated levels of the mind of the analyst who says "Oh well, I think you are cured" and finishes—in other words, runs away—or gets angry and says "Oh don't be so silly; don't be so ridiculous."

I think it is necessary to interpret the patient's relationship with himself. He isn't simply frightened of being eaten up by the analyst or the hospital; he is frightened of being eaten up by *himself*. For example, suppose the patient finds that masturbation has a very soothing effect and that the anxiety is somehow relieved by the stimulation of his own genitalia. Then comes the fear that the pleasures of masturbation will take possession of him, that he will go mad—a very common fear we come across where people are able to express feelings of fear of going mad but don't usually know why. It can generally be traced to their fear of a pleasurable or rewarding experience.

To revert to the point I made yesterday: the importance of the analyst's ability to provide the space in which he can develop. Whatever body of theory attracts you, you should also consider whether there is room in it for the expansion of yourself. You should not be afraid of these speculative imaginations and speculative reasons, which are extremely vulnerable and which can be destroyed with the slightest inclemency of weather, so to speak. If you find yourself speculating and imagining that this or the other story is relevant, you should allow yourself to entertain that speculation in the hope that it might grow into a communicable idea.

Q: May I ask Dr Bion if his suggested methodology, involving something in a constant state of renewal and ferment, or rather *in statu nascendi*, might be connected with the Eastern tradition, or have something in common with it? I'm thinking of the kind of teachings that gurus or yogis pass on to their followers. After all, what happened before strongly suggested this to me.

BION: I hope so, because I am somewhat distrustful of a method of treatment which suddenly springs out of the ground or springs out of the sky. I don't know why, but I have a prejudice in favour of acknowledging my indebtedness to my ancestors. I don't think I mind very much if I am accused of ancestor worship—I still would like to be able to acknowledge some sort of gratitude to my fore-bears.

Let us take a previous inhabitant of this city: he says, "Vixere fortes ante Agamemnona multi, sed omnes illacrimabiles urgentur ignotique longa nocte, carent quia vate sacro" [Many brave hearts lived before Agamemnon, but they drove to that long night unhonoured and unsung for lack of a sacred poet—Horace, *Odes*, IV: 9]. It is comforting to feel that our brilliant psychoanalytical theories are not necessarily a barrier which, while no doubt establishing our superiority to our ancestors, cuts us off from them for ever. I have no complaints about the complacency which is engendered by a feeling of success about achieving an analytic insight, but it is a great pity if it becomes ossified or fibrosed into a kind of impenetrable diaphragm which separates us for ever from our ancestors. If Horace could acknowledge the existence of poets long before him, I don't think there is any harm in our also acknowledging the existence of our predecessors even though they were never heard of.

Q: I'm pleased to say that, whereas yesterday Dr Bion was suggesting that we search for an object, today he has given us some coordinates, some positions, to help us get our bearings. So I wondered—to return to the people on the raft for a moment—whether something that might be useful to them is the idea of reversible perspective. It would be like providing them with an optical instrument to allow them to see more, rather than showing them an object. Let me give an example. In a group, there was a situation that went on for perhaps ten sessions where a girl spent the entire two hours of the session panting. Now (the whole thing was totally opaque to me at the time), from what has been said, it seems to me that what was needed was to find a different way of looking at the situation or, at any rate, first of all to overcome my inability to think. Later, when I realized it had to do with cowardice, I felt I could suggest to the group that it should look at the situation not from the medical and sacrificial point of view, but in terms of the impossibility of developing in a dimension of past and future. I merely wanted to add that it is an attempt to communicate.

BION: The analytic situation stimulates very primitive feelings, including the feelings of dependence and isolation; they are both unpleasant feelings. It is not, therefore, really surprising if one of the pair, and probably both, is aware that the psychoanalytic raft to which they cling in the consulting-room—beautifully disguised, of course, with comfortable chairs and every modern convenience—is nevertheless a very precarious raft in a tumultuous sea. Besides the various theories and interpretations to which the analyst gives expression, there needs to be an awareness that the two people are actually engaged in a dangerous adventure. There is always a tendency to snatch at some piece of material—some psychoanalytical theory or idea—as a kind of lifebelt which would help to keep the two feeling that they are still alive and floating. A common piece of wreckage is the idea of a "cure"; we snatch feverishly at the latest bit of cure that is available in order to keep afloat. That is something the analyst should be able to resist because, while it may have a temporarily curative effect, if it is constantly repeated then it becomes an addiction—the pair get addicted to cures. And in this peculiar sphere with which we are concerned, there are any amount of cures floating around. So it is a good thing if the analyst—in so far as he identifies himself with the responsible person—resists too many of these cheap cures which can be built into an elaborate structure so that, before you know where you are, the raft which is made of bits of wreckage turns into a delusional system which is a veritable *Titanic*. As we all know, the *Titanic* was unsinkable, it was the latest thing—but it hit up against a fact, and that sank it.

Mathematically, lines, circles and so on were profoundly changed by their translation into vectors, directions. I would suggest this: let us consider for the sake of argument that this experience here is a fact. Working our way back through speculative imaginations, speculative reasons, can we get back to the dream that we haven't had yet, tonight's dream, the dream which originates in the fact of this meeting? If we could do that, then we would be in a position to trace back the train of thought which might help to explain how it comes about that we are all in this room just now. This "fact" is one which ought to be classified as "incredible". If somebody wrote, or could write, the story of each individual member of this meeting and say they would meet in this particular room, in this particular hotel, at this particular date and time, anybody reading that story could only say, "How ridiculous!" There is no story which is so unbelievable as the true one.

Q: After the comment on the question of the ancestors and the quotation from Virgil and so on, I found myself thinking about yesterday's Freud quotation, in which he seemed to be emphasizing the continuity between intrauterine life and early infancy, rather than the caesura of birth, on which a lot of stress had been placed.

Now in Dr Bion's presentation yesterday, when he mentioned Otto Rank's concept of the birth trauma, I thought he was suggesting that we are "too impressed by the trauma of birth". On this point I disagreed with the interpreter, who interpreted that we are *not sufficiently* impressed by the birth trauma. Could you please enlarge on this point, as I don't want to make too much noise.

BION: I am not aware that I was stressing either being impressed or not being impressed by the caesura of birth. I wanted to suggest that the caesura of birth, the anatomical and physiological fact, has a dominant effect on our view of whether the mind also is born at the moment of physiological birth.

When you are in the state of mind of the person who is awake, with all your senses about you and conscious, what relation does what you *say* you dreamt have to the experience which you had when you were in a different state of mind—namely, the state of mind when you were asleep? I am sometimes told that the patient had a "dream" and that, for a fact, such-and-such happened. I am not so certain that "in fact" the patient dreamt it, nor am I so sure that the "facts" are as he described them. There are plenty of things we can call it: dream, delusion, hallucination and so on. The words have become so debased that they are virtually meaningless, and if they *are* given a meaning, that meaning is virtually useless. So it is hardly surprising if the patient we heard about earlier thinks that there is a lot to be said for the music. You may sometimes wonder why a patient comes to see you, and why the patient starts telling you whatever he tells you. As a step on the journey it may be quite useful to have an analyst who, the patient can say, thinks this or that—it is a relationship between two people. But it is really a relationship that the analysand has with the analysand. The highly intelligent embryo sees and experiences whatever it sees and experiences; the highly intelligent man or woman also gives a very convincing account of what is taking place. A difficulty would arise if by any chance we could introduce this highly intelligent postnatal person to the highly intelligent embryo who could tell such very different stories, different narratives about the same facts. If the "unsinkable" *Titanic* could meet with its passengers, those it sank, I wonder what the dialogue would be. If they met *before* that unfortunate fact, they could say, "I had a terrifying dream." One could reply, "Don't be so silly—it was only a dream." I leave it to you to imagine what they would say *afterwards*.

Rome, 10 July 1977

Q : I'd like to ask Dr Bion if he can tell us more about his ideas on the countertransference, because it seems to me that this is the particular type of noise in the analyst's mind that can be picked up in the psychoanalytic experience. I wonder if it might also contain musical elements, and if so if we should adjust our minds like a high-fidelity system that can not only extract the signal from the noise, but also act like a resonance chamber and allow us to receive the entire range of acoustic stimuli, even if that means that the clarity of the melody is lost.

BION: The idea of the transference and the countertransference has been extremely productive, provocative and growth-stimulating. But, like every really good idea, like anything which provokes or stimulates growth, it makes itself out of date at once. When individuals are exposed to the analytic experience for the first time, they don't understand what that experience is or what its name is. Nor does the analyst say, "You are experiencing transference to me"—that is a technical term which is useful for people who have already had the experience of psychoanalytic training. After a time, though, the novice begins to understand that the analyst is drawing attention to an actual experience which he is having. If he is becoming an analyst, then he may reach a point where we could say, "That is what we mean by transference—that is a transference manifestation. Your feeling that I am your father or mother can be compared with other ideas you have: you can bring together both the idea that I am your mother or father *and* the idea that I am a stranger whom you do not know. Then you can decide for yourself who or what you really think I am—that is your affair. In that way a new idea is born. The idea that you had before—namely, that I am a blood relation, a father or mother—is transient; it is a temporary idea on the journey of your life. From that point of view the technical term "transference" can be seen to have a resemblance to ordinary usage. It is an idea that you have "on the way"—you transfer it to me as a temporary measure on your way to what you really think or feel. At the same moment the new idea that you have is a temporary one and will be discarded sooner or later. It is another of these places where you stop on your own particular journey. If you could look at these various ideas which you have in the course of this experience with me, you might be able to trace a sort of map showing the stations of your journey from point A to point Z. Where you are now, when you have just seen this point, is already out of date."

Consequently I would say that the idea of transference and countertransference is hardly worth mentioning to this audience. That would be suitable if we were concerned with writing the history of psychoanalysis; then it might be interesting to say, "Transference, as defined by Freud is . . . Transference, as defined by Abraham is . . . Transference, as defined by Melanie Klein is . . .". In short, may I hand you the Encyclopaedia of Psycho-Analysis. You will find all the definitions laid down here if you want to know the history. But if you are, in fact, having a psychoanalytic experience—that is different.

Nansen was asked, "How did you get to the Pole?" His reply was something like this [draws on the blackboard], "That's my route." That is a pictorial representation of how Nansen discovered the North Pole; that is how he got there; there's the map. He drew it much better than I have—although he had just had a very good dinner. In the actual experience of analysis there isn't time to do that; there isn't time to carry out this sort of discussion. Once the patient begins to understand what the analytic experience is, then he changes so fast that what he thought or felt at the beginning of a sentence is out of date by the time he has reached the end of it. That is why, when you are satisfied that the patient is actually developing, it is as well to be able to forget what you know and to discard what you want to happen. It is difficult to de-barrass the mind of its load of experience; we are liable to slow the patient down by clinging to out-of-date ideas and, as a result, are unable to watch the patient's progress to some other idea.

As I said yesterday, I think it is as well to be able to acknowledge our debt to our ancestors—our mental ancestors. It is quite appropriate for us, as analysts, to know what was meant by "transference" or "countertransference" when used by Freud, Abraham, Melanie Klein or anybody else, only if at the same time we learn how to forget it all so as to be open to the next move which is made by the patient—the next stopping station, as it were.

The patient who has very gifted genetic ancestry—a very intelligent father and mother—is the product of what the biologists call "sexual relationship" between that particular father and mother and therefore develops from a germ which has chromosomes derived from both parties. If the development is adequately expressed in physical terms, then it can be worked out in terms of that sort of inheritance. But if there is such a thing as a mind or spirit or soul, that may not follow the same laws as those of Mendelian inheritance. As psychoanalysts who believe in the existence of a mind, we then have to consider what are the laws of inheritance of the mind. Provisionally, transiently, on the way to something better, I would like to suggest something like "phenotypes" as contrasted with "genotypes". By supposing something of that sort, we might be able to work out the laws of, the inheritance of, acquired characteristics, which according to Mendelian theory are not transmitted. I suppose the existence of speculative imagination, speculative reasons, for the early development of those characteristics which are mental, which, as I have already suggested, have a different form of inheritance from that of the genotypes.

Every single one of us would be hard put to it to write down his or her mental journey and mental inheritance. Who or what were

your ancestors? I don't want to hear about your genetic ancestors—
what are the other ones? Could you have a look at your character or
personality, this queer thing which I am sure exists? I am convinced from my experience—partly as an analyst, but on the whole
through life—that there *is* such a thing as a character or a mind. I
don't think I am always affected by the physical appearance of the
person, although, thanks to the dominance of our eyes, the cosmetic element is likely to play a very big part and we can immediately be affected by the feeling of liking or disliking somebody. We
don't even have to go deeper than skin-deep, literally or metaphorically: "I don't like that person—he's white" (or "black"). It
would be a ridiculous situation if a doctor refused to examine a
patient who had a cachectic flush or showed signs of inflammation
or of jaundice. As doctors we are expected not to take such a
prejudiced view of what the body tells us, because our examination
of that body is supposed to be more than skin-deep. The situation is
not so very different if we are supposed to be concerned with the
human mind or character or personality. If we are sensitive to this
supposed "thing", then the fact that we don't like that person—or
that character or that personality—is irrelevant. We are nevertheless supposed to know some more about that character or personality, whether we like it or not.

As analysts we have to be disciplined to a situation where,
whatever the facts are, we do not allow them to make us run away
or do the opposite—fall in love. We are supposed still to remain
analysts. We are not obliged to become inhuman people who
cannot love or hate: we are still supposed to retain the capacity to
have feelings of love and hate and all the other feelings which go
with them, but at the same time we are supposed to remain disciplined. To take an extreme example such as battle action: an officer
is not supposed to be afraid, but that does not mean that he does
not know that a situation is dangerous. Nor yet is he supposed to
be so carried away by a victory as to assume that the war is over.
That is one reason why I suggested last time that we are surrounded by the wreckage of cures all over the place—the remains
of the wreckage of the disaster in which somebody has been sunk
by cure, sunk by his desires, misled by his hopes and fears—
whichever part is showing above the surface, like the iceberg. As

the poet [Arthur Clough (1819–1861)] says, "If hopes were dupes, fears may be liars."

Have we any coordinate system which could give us an idea as to where we are, where the pair are—the analyst and the patient? In the narrative story we can get an idea of a person's development by taking any two points, A and B, and the direction would be from A to B. Those two points, A and B, we could call "real and distinct". However, suppose those two points were mobile; then they might travel round the circumference of a circle and become "real and coincident", And if we try to draw in the two points which are real and coincident, we can say that they meet and describe a line which is a tangent.

Take these two people—the analyst and the analysand—who have met at one point. I don't know what spiritual route the analyst has taken, the journey that his mind has taken between the point at which it is supposed it began its existence and the point at which it became coincident with an entirely different personality—coincident and real. Let us suppose that these two points go on with their journey: the analyst and analysand continue to live; they don't stop at psychoanalysis; they don't stop at this point at which they are real and coincident. I was taught to call that "conjugate complex". I didn't have—and still haven't—any particular ideas about what to translate that into. I am glad to find that even my translator here had to hesitate for a moment. However, I use these two words "conjugate complex" as imaginary points. I am assured—and I hope there is a mathematician here who can inform me more correctly—that these imaginary points still obey the laws of real ones. In that way I think we ought to consider, as if it were real, that the analyst and analysand still continue to exist even when the analysis is over, when those two points, which are real and distinct, real and coincident in the analyst's consulting-room, continue in a space about which I know nothing because that mind which is no longer in contact with me has gone I don't know where.

Q: Thinking of this alchemy of human existences and encounters between thoughts, I wonder if Dr Bion can explain to me the role of the human need to know—what I think he calls K. And, second, what part is played in the patient by the need to express his desire for knowledge to someone?

BION: I suspect that these are vestiges of fundamental characteristics which have not yet been destroyed either by the inability to tolerate ignorance or by the inability to tolerate the answer. The trouble about curiosity is that it is liable to provoke a response. From what I know of myself, the danger to which anybody exposes themselves by asking me a question is another flood of questions. I do try to resist the temptation to say, "Yes, I know; I know about transference; I know about countertransference." I am partly assisted by the fact that I *don't* know. That picture in which Nansen showed exactly how he got to the North Pole does not tell me—and I would never know—what it would be like to be Nansen wandering in the wastes of the Arctic. I only know a little bit about what it feels like to be me wandering in the realms of the human mind. One hopes that it is a relatively limited sphere—not quite so dangerous, perhaps, as wandering in the realms of omniscience or omnipotence. There are various pictorial images, narrative images, fables, in which it is supposed that the attempt to eat of the forbidden fruit of the Tree of Wisdom excited the highly dangerous wrath of omnipotence and omniscience. To be dominated or motivated by curiosity, by our wish to know, would seem to be a dangerous occupation, especially if we come across another mind which has the characteristic of omniscience or omnipotence. As Milton put it, "who durst defy th'Omnipotent to arms" [*Paradise Lost*, Bk. I]. As analysts we may be always running the risk of questioning whoever or whatever is clothed in authority. It is not only the psychoanalytic investigation which is suspect, but also any activity which might be seen as arming ourselves by improving such minds or instruments as we have available for investigating the unknown.

Q: Let me take up Dr Bion's image of the analytic couple who meet at a certain time at a real, coincident point and later split up, so that each, as it were, goes off at a tangent. Dr Bion says that the couple nevertheless continues to exist, but he doesn't know how and where. I wondered if what happens is the transformation of a relationship which, as between the analysand and the analyst, is an object relationship, and if this object, which goes off at a tangent, later becomes a spatialized object—if it becomes an area or a space. And this applies to the analysand as well as to the analyst. In other words, I wanted to ask Dr Bion what relation there is between a relationship with a real object and one with a spatialized object.

BION: I doubt whether any of us would ever know, because we are so ephemeral, so short-lived. One feels that we, this group, have some existence previous to this meeting. You can put any number of years to it if you consider that the calendar gives you an adequate measure to go by. But a few orbits of the earth around the sun is a very insignificant method of counting time. Similarly, the distance from Los Angeles to Rome is too small. So the measurements of both time and space are simply not adequate. These two "things"—I have to borrow from the language of material objects—leave the consulting-room and go out into space and time. It is difficult enough to find a coordinate of geometrical space; it took several hundred years before the Cartesian coordinates were produced, and then really by accident. The coordinates of the time and space into which these two characters or souls or personalities—again, I am not even able to give a precise name to it—are launched are very difficult to describe. Even our imagination is not free if we try to imagine what would be occupying this space, here, in the relatively insignificant time of two thousand years ago, who or what was occupying what we now call "Rome". But the same thing applies to this space which is occupied by "Rome" and what it will have turned into in two thousand years' time—which, as I say, is a relatively insignificant time span. As far as absolute space is concerned, the astronomers imagine that the solar system will have completed its journey when it has made one revolution around the galactic centre. The most recent estimate that I have heard is that the diameter is something like 10^8 million light-years—quite a long time. Nevertheless, I suppose we can add some minute bit of knowledge to this problem of the coordinates by which we could plot the course of these two people when they leave the consulting-room.

I would like to mention an example, which I have often used, of the kind of thing that I mean. Hugh Kenner was talking to a yokel in Warwickshire and mentioned how beautiful the dandelions looked. The yokel replied, "Yes, we call them golden boys and girls, and later when the petals fall off, we call them chimney-sweepers." Hugh Kenner was familiar with a song from *Cymbeline*, two lines of which are, "Golden lads and girls all must, / As chimney-sweepers, come to dust." The Warwickshire yokel, without any education, was using a language which must have been commonplace in Shakespeare's time. So Shakespeare may have been making a commonplace remark—"as chimney-sweepers come to dust". I don't know what Shakespeare could have been thinking . . .

[*The remainder of this seminar is missing from the recording.*]

Rome, 13 July 1977

In some ways it is an advantage to me to know that I don't know any Italian, because I think you can be misled by thinking you *do* know Italian. Patients *seem* to talk French, or English or Italian, but what *we* want to hear is not any of those languages. I find it difficult to say what language we need to listen to; the nearest I can get to it is to say that it is the language of what Freud would call "the unconscious".

I have seen this stated most clearly recently by Dr Matte Blanco, who mentions this peculiar fact of Freud sometimes talking about "the unconscious", and at other times talking about something as "unconscious". They are two different things. Furthermore, I have come across material which seems never to have been what Freud would have called "conscious". Dr Segal described a situation in which a patient says it is obvious that somebody who is playing the violin is masturbating. I had a patient who, I began to feel, wore his mind inside out—that is to say, like clothes worn inside out: what ought to be on the inside is on the outside. Falling back on metaphorical language, I could say that the patient behaved as if his unconscious was outside. So the interpretations which we would think appropriate formulations of unconscious thoughts and ideas are, in fact, ordinary statements to the patient. He has no difficulty whatever in thinking that the analyst is saying things which are obvious. On the other hand, if we resort to ordinary speech, waking thought, conscious thought, the patient says, "I don't know what you mean." He has no difficulty in understanding a psychoanalytic interpretation of something we could regard as "unconscious", but he cannot understand the language we talk when we are wide awake, fully conscious and aware of what we call the "facts", "reality".

I used to find this difficult to understand—I still do. I also found that it made me angry. I thought I preserved a disciplined attitude and was quite polite, but the patient had no difficulty at all in knowing that I was annoyed. That was also annoying—I didn't like being analysed by my patient. But I persisted, and so did the patient.

After a time I drew the patient's attention to the fact that he had not said why he came to me or what he wanted me to do. His reply was, "I have been telling you all the time. You mean to say you don't know now?" Well, I didn't. I felt I had to do a lot of thinking about this extraordinary situation. Why did the patient keep on coming? I didn't know.

Another patient complained strongly about the behaviour of everybody else. Thinking of this in terms of projection, I tried to draw his attention to the fact that everybody was wrong, but that there was nothing wrong with him. There again, thinking over the matter, I couldn't understand why he kept on coming. If the situation was that A, B, C, D and so on were so hostile and so difficult, what was I supposed to do? What was I supposed to interpret? There is nothing I can do about a universe in which everybody is wrong. The inhabitants of this world don't all come to me for analysis; the one person who does come has nothing the matter with him.

I searched my mind in the hope of finding some interpretation which would appear to approximate to this situation. I thought of the various interpretations which Freud gives—particularly those dealing with *the* unconscious, the repression of conscious ideas, the filling of the gap, the space occupied by amnesia, by paramnesias—but it wasn't any good. I thought of Melanie Klein's idea of projective identification—an "omnipotent phantasy" that the patient believes he can evacuate his thoughts which are out of control but which nevertheless persecute him. I gave various interpretations in accordance with that theory. I couldn't see that it had any effect whatsoever. So the problem was, is psychoanalysis any use at all? Why give these interpretations—Freudian, Abrahamian, Kleinian and so forth—none of which has any effect at all?

It seems to me that the one essential in analysis is that we should be able to go on thinking in a situation which is extremely tense. We are bound to be anxious about our ability to treat and, at the same time, about our apparent inability to do anything about the fact that either the theories of psychoanalysis are wrong, or the idea that the correct interpretation will cure the patient is wrong, or that something else which we do not know is wrong—or all of them.

I would like to continue the discussion in a way more applicable to what we want to know or think about before seeing tomorrow's patient. I shall be glad to try to go on from there on any theme that you wish to introduce. I could sum up the question by saying, "Where do we go from here?"

Q: Dr Bion's comments on nonverbal communication put me in mind of something that Paul Valéry said: that the entire substance of what people say lies in song and in the sound of a voice, yet these are often disregarded, neglected. I'd like to connect this with the problem of distance and time in analytical work—when we might be either too close to the patient or too far away from him, and when we might say something either too soon or too late. As to the patient mentioned by Dr Bion who asks "What do you think of this?", I would ask a question: from his own experience, can he give us an example of a situation in which he answered immediately and another where he felt it was better to wait?

BION: The question goes to the root of the problem—namely, what is the space or time that we are talking about and are in? What coordinates can we suggest for locating the source or origin of the difficulty?

Can we observe the "thing itself"? Milton says in *Paradise Lost* [Bk. III],

So much the rather thou Celestial Light
Shine inward, and the mind through all her powers
Irradiate, there plant eyes, all mist from thence
Purge and disperse, that I may see and tell
Of things invisible to mortal sight.

We are mere mortals, mere human beings, so how are our minds to be irradiated by celestial light so that through all their powers they are illuminated, enabling us to see (first point) and tell (second point) of things invisible to mortal sight? Our problem tomorrow is, how are we to see, observe—which is regarded, in any case, as the first requisite of a scientific outlook—these things which are not visible? How are we to see the invisible and then formulate what we see in such a way that the patient can see what we want him to see. There are two points: the first is to be able to see it ourselves; the second, to find a mode of communication so that we can tell the patient.

Are we able to be scientific at all in the sense of observing the facts? Up to a point we can. We may have a patient who is flushed: in other words, in so far as his body is communicating and if we have enough medical experience and training, we are able to observe a flushed appearance on the cheeks of the patient which a lay person couldn't see. We can teach medical students how to observe. We say, "You must examine the patient; you must look at him; you must ask him to remove his clothes so that you can palpate his body and in that way understand the language spoken by the body—that is, diagnose the condition." It doesn't seem to me that that is in any way different from the analyst who is trying to interpret the mind. Physically we call it "diagnosis"; analytically we call it "interpretation".

In saying that, I have made an entirely artificial separation; I have talked about the body and the mind as if they were two entirely different things. I don't believe it. I think that the patient whom you see tomorrow is one, a whole, a complete person. And although we say—obeying the laws of grammar—that we can observe his body and mind, in fact there is no such thing as a "body and mind"; there is a "he" or a "she".

To take up this other point about distance: what is the distance between "there" and "here"? What is the distance between the state of mind which is repressed and the state of mind which has done the repressing?

The same thing, put in a different way: what is the distance between the person, awake and conscious, who says, "I had a dream last night", and the person who, in a different state of mind, experienced the dream? Suppose the sleeping person is restless, twists and turns because he is aware of a pain. It may be because he has appendicitis, or it may be because he has painful thoughts or ideas. When he tells us that he had a bad dream, where do you locate the discomfort? Is the source of that discomfort physical? Or is it what we call "mental"?

That is your problem tomorrow and all the other tomorrows. The only person who knows the answer to that question is your patient. Therefore he is the one collaborator on whom you can really rely.

If the patient is suffering from leukaemia, he doesn't know enough to understand what his body is telling him; he is dependent on a doctor, or a psychoanalyst, or both. A doctor, if he is well-versed in medicine, and if he knows how to observe, can see that there is an infection, something producing an inflammation; that is what his patient's body tells him. What are psychoanalysts to observe? How are they to be aware of these pains? And, then, how are they to see them—the total situation, body *and* mind, one person? In the consulting-room the analyst is all alone; he can depend only on such powers of observation as he has and on the patient. Similarly, the patient has nobody on whom to depend except the analyst. Therefore this *practical* situation, the *practice* of psychoanalysis, involves the relationship between two people—but, half a minute: is it only between two people? Anatomically, physically, there are A and B. Is that real? Are there only two people? If we look at and listen to what is in the room, what shall we look at? The patient? Our own free associations? Our own ideas as to what this is? Or a *relationship* between two people? It is *at least* two people. Is it what Dr Matte Blanco calls a "symmetrical relationship"? Or is it something else? That seems to me to be a matter which can only be decided by us who practise psychoanalysis. It is no good looking at books about psychoanalysis—there is no time. This has to be observed in your session tomorrow.

Perhaps somebody here could formulate the nature of this problem still further. I think it is a mistaken idea that there is some analyst who knows the answers. I now know quite enough to know that I don't know. And in spite of all the pressure to which I am subjected to know the answers, I *don't* know them. But I am sure that between us all we may learn a bit more and be a bit wiser by tomorrow evening.

Q: The problem of communication and non-communication—the aspect of the limits of communicability—centres on the patient rather than on the analytic relationship. Otherwise it might be possible to do something about the different potentials of certain analytic couples for development, which sometimes favour the development of the analyst as well as the patient. Here one really feels that the things that are developed are very close to primary repression—aspects that have never benefited from contact with reality. This potential often impresses its stamp even on the intake session, so that the analyst sometimes feels compelled to take on a patient he had not previously thought of accepting for analysis. Perhaps it is precisely this situation which results in analyses that are productive for analyst and patient alike.

BION: No one should set up as an analyst or doctor unless he is prepared to pay the price. To put it in other words, "If you can't stand the heat, keep out of the kitchen." Once you want to help your fellow men and women, you are in trouble. It doesn't matter how ill you are, how tired, how mentally or physically sick, you have to preserve your discipline. I gave the example of getting angry with a patient. It doesn't fool the patient. That is *not* good behaviour on the part of the analyst—he has to continue to behave in a civilized manner.

To take a more extreme situation: the officer in war whose troops are frightened and want to run away. The officer is not privileged to run away too. His privilege is to stay where he is, even if it costs him his life. That may seem to be an exaggerated description of your session tomorrow with your patient. I don't believe it. I think it is hidden because the psychoanalyst's consulting-room is comfortable, he has good food, and so on. But he can be so overwhelmed with noise—putting it again metaphorically—that it is difficult to hear. The noise comes from within—hypotheses about physical illnesses, hypotheses about analytic theories—masses of them ad infinitum. They all make such a noise that it is difficult to hear what the patient's body and mind are saying. I have tried to put this rather crudely as divesting our minds of memory and desire so that the noise made by our learning, our training, our past experience, is at a minimum. In that way you get as wide a view as possible. Then you can begin to hear or feel something which, if it were an inflammation, would cause you to narrow down your view to the site of the infection so that you could look at this spot which is painful. If your patient will allow you to see him often enough, if he will allow you to remain silent, if he will allow you to be ignorant, then you may be able to see what this painful spot is—whether it is in the mind or the body.

In saying all that, I am talking about matters which have not yet been discovered; nobody can help you there except you and your patient between you tomorrow. A physician would have to dare to say, "I shall want to see you tomorrow; I don't know what is the matter, but I think it *may* be going to be an appendicitis, or it may be nothing in particular." The analyst can observe the body, the appearance of the patient, *and* can observe what appears to be a symptom or a sign that the patient has a mind. The capacity for articulate speech can be observed, can be searched, can be looked at so that it might yield evidence of the location of the pain. I suspect that sometimes a physical pain—say, below the diaphragm—can seep its way up to the mind so that the symptom, the sign, which is not so obvious in the body can be observed in the mind. Then the analyst may be able to make an interpretation which a physician cannot make because he hasn't learnt how to observe the mind.

As I have said, the occupation of psychoanalysis is a dangerous one, but the analyst cannot deal with that dangerous situation by running away from it. We all know that; we all know it would be no good getting up and leaving the room. What is not quite so easy to see is that we can become *absent in mind* if we don't like what the patient is saying. In my experience, the borderline psychotic patient—so-called—always knows when the analyst has become absent in mind. Sometimes the patient will say, "You have gone away", and it is easy enough to give an interpretation such as, "Ah yes, you are aware that it is coming up to the week-end break—I shan't see you tomorrow or the day after." It is a rational explanation—and in analysis rational explanations are so common that there is no shortage. We can produce interpretations, clothe ourselves with interpretations which hide our nakedness. Not so with the borderline psychotic. The problem is, are you going to interpret the patient's statement as his reaction to the week-end break or the termination of analysis? Or are you going to interpret, "You are feeling that I am not really paying attention"? This is the penalty which the analyst pays for being an analyst—he is under constant observation. Unless we are aware of that, we don't know why we get so tired.

A greedy patient can behave in such a way that when his hour is over, you are so bothered about what he will get up to next that you take up the next patient's time in thinking about the previous patient. I think it is as well to be clear about this: that you will try to prevent the patient, say, from throwing himself out of the window while he is in your consulting-room during that hour. After that you can say that you will not be responsible: somebody will have to bring the patient to your office, and somebody will have to take that patient away—whether it is a child or an adult, psychotic or non-psychotic. Otherwise, the other patients during the day are cheated; the attention which the analyst ought to be devoting to the observation of all his patients is spent on thought about what this one patient will do. You cannot work twenty-four hours a day: only you can say how many hours you can work, only you can arrange the conditions so that, during those hours, the conditions enable you to work because your attention is not distracted by matters that take you away from the job in hand.

Let me remind you again that this is why I think it is important to be able to denude your mind either of what you know about the past or of your desires for the future. The whole of psychoanalysis seems to me to be shot through with a certain optimism—these ideas of "cure", that there's a good time coming. What do we know about what is coming? What do we know about this universe in which we live? It is possible that the patient needs to be stronger and more disciplined in order to be ready for whatever happens— not just prepared for heaven, a cure which is heaven-on-earth.

One idea we can pursue is that of the truth. You can feel that a painter is a good painter if his painting is an attempt to show you what is true—the Impressionists didn't paint in order to make things more difficult to see. You can feel the difference between a musical composition which is an imitation of the truth and another which is a formulation of the truth. In analysis we have to forget whether the interpretation is the right interpretation, or the Kleinian interpretation, or the Freudian interpretation—it is all irrelevant. The only relevant thing is whether it is a *true* interpretation. This is illustrated with dramatic force if you are asked to see a patient who is in the terminal stages of disease. The doctor can expect the analyst to tell the patient reassuring stories: the analyst has to resist that pressure. I don't think such a patient is misled about his condition—although it is possible, because we are all so used to believing nonsense of one sort or another, of being told reassuring stories. A patient will sometimes say, "I don't know what you mean"—he doesn't believe that the analyst is in any way different from everybody else. He thinks it very unlikely that the analyst will say just what he means. But the analyst has to get so accustomed to saying what he means that he does so *always*—however unpleasant it may be. He cannot think, "Ah yes, X is the right interpretation, but I will say something nicer." He must ask himself, "What language shall I talk to the patient so that he can understand what I say?"

It is possible to feel that in certain patients, ideas, thoughts and feelings are prompted from a basic physical level—for example, prompted by the adrenals or by the gonads. Can the impulse, thought or feeling that comes up from a physical source affect the mind and thoughts of the patient? Can that same mind be told something in language which can track its way back again to these primitive, fundamental levels?

I had a patient who submitted to surgery for a heart condition. Whether the operation was really carried out or simply an incision made on the skin, I don't know. For all I know, it may have been a psychological incision. But I do know that the operation was not successful. I had to draw the patient's attention to the fact that there must be some reason why he kept coming to me when his heart had been operated on—or so he told me—and that he must know that all I ever did was talk. Yet that patient, who hadn't dared to travel, began to do so. *I* hadn't operated on his heart and I don't know what happened to my interpretations once I had given them. The impression I got was that the patient did listen to what I said— but what happened from his ears to his mind I don't know.

These are problems which we may be able to solve if people come to see us; you may gradually feel—tomorrow, the day after— that there is some evidence which begins to formulate itself in the same way that an obscurity on an X-ray film shows you a pattern. If you know what the skeleton of the chest ought to look like, then you can see on an X-ray film that there is an area of opacity; where a photograph of the skeleton ought to emerge, there is a misty patch. So getting back—or forward—to tomorrow's patient, I suggest this view where you are vulnerable to anything that your senses will tell you: as you watch, you begin to narrow it down, and then ask yourself why you are acting in that way. That depends on daring to feel or think whatever you feel or think. I have spoken of it before as a situation in which all sorts of thoughts are flying around—the patient gets rid of all his thoughts which then, in my pictorial imagination, are flying around. If you can be wide open, then I think there is a chance that you might catch some of those wild thoughts. And if you allow them to lodge in your mind, however ridiculous, however stupid, however fantastic, then there may be a chance of having a look at them. That is a matter of daring to have such thoughts—never mind whether you are supposed to have them or not—and keeping them long enough to be able to formulate what they are.

Q: I wondered what space we should be looking into: might it perhaps be a mental space that can also gradually be built up? And, then, what might a space for looking inside ourselves be worth?

BION: Projective geometry is implicit in Euclidean geometry, but it took a very long time before Descartes was able to formulate the Cartesian coordinates. Then, released from the pictorial image of lines, circles, points, it could be formulated in terms which were not visible. It is possible to formulate things like conic sections mentally—and not only the lines, but the *direction* of the lines: vectors.

What about these thoughts that float up, shall we say, from the adrenals? Could we discover some kind of coordinate system by which it would be possible to observe them going in the other direction? To take my pictorial example of a hand, one side being psycho-somatic, the other soma-psychotic: if you can give an interpretation about a psycho-somatic condition, could you also give an interpretation in such a way that it would be soma-psychotic? In that way, these puzzling things like schizophrenias, manic-depressives and so on could become much more comprehensible. Consider "manic-depressive": manic husband marries depressive wife, and they thus give birth to a *folie à deux*. Could we put it in the other direction? Start at the *folie à deux* and end up with two people? And would they remain married?

Q: There is some confusion here in the translation: are we, in fact, talking about "soma-psychotic", or should it be "soma-psychic"?

BION: They are different views of the same thing—it is a sort of diaphragm, a caesura, the "impressive caesura of birth". There are plenty of impressive caesuras of the birth of ideas, and each time somebody has a new idea—for example, psychoanalysis—it at once becomes a barrier, something which is difficult to penetrate. Instead of being liberating, it becomes imprisoning. So even while we try to formulate an idea which would be liberating, we formulate yet another caesura which is liable to become impenetrable.

Rome, 15 July 1977

I don't know "us", and I don't think that we know "us" either, because we—whoever we are—have not met before. We are none of us who we were even an hour ago, so I shall start by having a speculative imagination, something that is *not* a fact, an imaginary fact. When there are a lot of individuals here, there are also a lot of thoughts without a thinker, and these thoughts-without-a-thinker are floating around somewhere. I suggest that they are looking for a thinker. I hope that some of you will be prepared to allow them a lodgement in your minds or personalities. I realize that that is asking a lot, because these thoughts-without-a-thinker, these stray thoughts, are liable also to be wild thoughts. And nobody likes giving a home to wild thoughts which are then said to be *your* thoughts. We all like our thoughts to be domesticated; we like them to be civilized thoughts, well-trained, rational thoughts. All the same, however wild, however irrational, these thoughts may be, I hope that you will dare to give them a temporary lodgement and that you will then provide them with a suitable verbal costume so that they can express themselves publicly and be given an airing even if they do not appear to be very well fitted out. I hope that these speculative imaginations will have a chance of achieving a certain degree of respectability, so that they can exist even in a scientific community. Like speculative reasons, they are feeble creatures, easily destroyed.

I find from time to time a patient who says that he is incapable of imagination. In such circumstances I am not surprised if that same person complains of insomnia. Such people are afraid that they will be off their guard as they are when they go to sleep. When they *are* able to go to sleep and to have dreams, they say they have had a dream because a dream is relatively respectable; we are permitted to have dreams. It is not regarded as quite so respectable to have a hallucination or a delusion, although sometimes the society or group or the culture allows people to have daydreams. Usually an attempt is made to make these daydreams respectable by excusing them as a poem, or an impressionist painting or a modern musical composition. But that again depends on daring to have a wild thought, whether awake or asleep. And it depends on being able to wake up, to be fully conscious, to have all your wits about you, and then to be able to transform the wild thought or the wild image so that it becomes relatively respectable, so that you can say, "It's a field of poppies."

Sometimes such people are forgiven, especially if they are dead. Then you can say, "After all, it was Giotto, or Leonardo." People like that can be excused if they drew a line around their wild thought and called it "God", or "The Virgin Mary", or "Saint Anne". But most of us hardly dare to hope that we shall be able to make that excuse for our wild thoughts, wild images, wild music or wild paintings. So when I say to you, "I think somebody else ought to do some talking, however wild the thought, however irrational, however unaccepted or unacceptable or unthinkable to the group or person", I am really expecting you to be courageous. That point is difficult to see, because apparently and factually the circumstances are quite comfortable; it sounds and looks and feels as if it is safe to say what you think.

I try to speak the truth to my patients and to dare to say what I think, even though I have to modify it slightly because I want them to understand what I have said. Sometimes the patient will say, "I don't know what you mean." This may be because I am not good at expressing myself in articulate speech, but often it is because the patient is not used to hearing somebody say what he means. So here you run the risk of being regarded as responsible for your wild thoughts, and then you run the risk that somebody will say, "That person is a trouble-maker."

If I now fall silent, it is in the hope that you will be able to hear yourselves think, however wild the thought is, even to yourself. There is always one person who can hear what you think—and that is you. [*Long silence.*] You can hear the clamour yourselves. The group seems to me to be suffering from insomnia.

Q: In a report I read about life in Persia today, the journalist said that the principle followed by most of the population is that everyone is the slave of what he has said and master of the words he has not said. Now it seems to me that the opposite may also be the case—that is, that a person is the master, the owner, of what he has said and may, in fact, be the slave or prisoner of what he doesn't say. In such a situation, it seems to me that if someone thinks something, there may be someone who does not think or whose thinking is confused; at least he has a path of his own to follow. Alternatively, there is the situation of someone who thinks but doesn't express what he thinks. That puts me in mind of a pregnancy in which the foetus is likely to die if it is born too soon, because it is too weak and not fit to live. In the same way, if a thought is not expressed, if it is immature, it will not survive; it won't go very far. But if the foetus stays in the mother's body for too long, it will die inside, just as a thought will die in the throat if it is held back for too long.

BION: The idea has been expressed, as I said the other day, by a previous inhabitant of this city, Horace [see Seminar 2]. Think of the first people who started to communicate with grunts and then dared to invent articulate speech; they had to be their own poets. You have to dare to be an artist; somebody has to dare to write graffiti on the walls of the cave. What those artists were called, I don't know. They were not called "Homer" or "Leonardo", and yet their terrifying dreams are there on the walls of the cave. Their terrifying sculptures are visible in the caves of Elephanta. The first attempts must have been very crude. What about the graffiti now, the drawings which appear on the walls of Rome? In the Lascaux caves I have seen the uneven surface of the wall used to produce an effect of perspective; that sculpture has been achieved by a collaboration between a human character, personality, and the forces of nature; the earth bulges out in a certain place and the artist uses that as a part of his sculpture.

But never mind the past; we can do nothing about that. What we can do something about is the present. Faced with a choice, you always choose both what to do *and* what not to do. I can choose to do that, and I can choose to do that, meaning "I choose this, not that".

Here, now, dare you express your creation, make it public—at any rate to yourself, because you are bound to hear? Somebody once collected the bits of paper left after a meeting of important statesmen; their scribbles on pieces of paper would not have been accepted by a museum of modern art. If you decide to remain silent, then you are also deciding not to say what you could have said; you are bound to regret not having spoken up, and you are bound to regret having been so foolish as to have said what you were thinking.

Q: I'd like to put to Dr Bion an attempt of mine to use speculative imagination. In so far as a cell membrane separates an inside from an outside and selects the distribution of the cellular substances into two parts of the space, we can say that the membrane sends a remote message and organizes the space in a more complex way than would be possible if the molecules were scattered at random. As the complexity of the functional aggregation (an organ, for example) increases, so too do the interdependences and complexity of the relations that must be maintained between the inside of the organ and other regions of the organism. For example, the adrenal gland will be separated from a surrounding space by a sheath, but this sheath will have lost the property of maintaining functional relations with the outside, as the cell membrane did. The function of an organizer capable of acting at a distance will now be assumed by the system of adrenal secretions and specific receptors for these substances, which are located outside the adrenal gland (in the pituitary, say). In other words, new membranes are created to regulate exchanges, and these are no longer located at a single point in space and do not act by contiguity. So in effect we have membrane systems capable of acting at greater distances with less transport of substances.

My question is this: Considering these examples, do you think it useful to see evolution as a series of functional leaps that tend to preserve homoeostasis in a system whose growing complexity gives rise to ever-increasing dishomogeneity between the various regions of the space and, for this purpose, needs regulating systems capable of acting over greater and greater distances? Do you feel that this can throw any light on the fact that the senses are a membrane capable of acting at a greater distance between two inhomogeneous entities such as the body and the external environment, by forging a relationship between substances originating in the systems that act at short distances (hormonal stimuli or emotions) and receptors in the far-off mind of the mother?

Could it be that the birth of thought here serves as a membrane that can actually interpose itself for action at a distance between individual substances and social receptor systems?

BION: The physiologists—I don't know with what degree of accuracy—describe the relationship of the cell to the extracellular fluid, which is as near to unpolluted water as you are ever likely to get. This makes it easier for me to reply to a part of what the previous speaker said. I can imagine—again, a speculative imagination— that, living in a watery fluid, a potentially highly gifted creature, an embryo, would not be able to tolerate what its primordial senses tell it. For example, it might hate the noise of the blood rushing through its embryonic body.

For the sake of simplicity I will mention an exaggerated case which nevertheless is factual—as far as I know. The mother, while pregnant, was subjected to a terrifying experience. What changes in pressure occurred in the amniotic fluid, I can only guess. And what those changes in pressure would be perceived as by the optic and auditory pits, I don't know. I am still postulating the possibility that the embryo, which has all the mental and physical makings, can be precociously, prematurely subjected to an experience which it cannot tolerate. The actual experience that I am acquainted with was that of a patient of mine who had severe symptoms. When he was a full-term foetus, a man entered the bedroom. He murdered the father, the mother, and three children and precipitated the premature birth of this full-term foetus. The child grew up and knew . . . well, what? I don't know. But everybody agreed that the child knew nothing about it, that it was not told, never had been told of this terrifying event. When I knew the patient, he was disapproved of by everybody, including the foster-parents. The patient had no dreams. After being subjected to the analytic experience with me, he became—and everybody was in agreement— infinitely worse. He had terrifying dreams; he was delinquent; he hated any man or woman that he had to deal with; he threatened murder and suicide. Naturally he was removed from the bad influence of the analyst; obviously analysis was doing the wrong thing and so was the analyst. So I could do nothing more. But the patient, when he was of age, came back to me. He didn't know what he wanted, but he knew he wanted me. That seems to be a situation in which the person, even before birth, is prematurely subjected to a stress which he cannot stand.

I have had other, less dramatic experiences in the analysis of patients who had been psychiatrically diagnosed as schizophrenic and borderline psychotic. I have three examples in mind: the root trouble appeared to me to be the great intelligence of all three people. I couldn't very well pass on the fact that, to me at any rate, they were highly intelligent people, but it was possible in two instances to draw the patients' attention to vestiges of acute observation—so acute that they could not stand the information that their primordial senses brought them.

There is one fundamental experience which I can put in this way: the patient is aware of two very unpleasant experiences— being dependent on something not himself *and* being all alone— both at the same time. That seems to me to be something which can happen even before birth when the patient is, as it were, aware of his dependence on a watery fluid and his inability to tolerate being all alone.

Ordinarily we are able to continue to operate our sense of smell by taking the watery fluid with us after birth, after entering into a gaseous fluid; the watery secretion of our nostrils enables us still to be able to smell, even in a gaseous medium. Sometimes there is too much watery fluid; we complain that we cannot breathe, we have catarrh—what is potentially an asset becomes a liability. Similarly, the patient cannot stand the load of intelligence he has to carry; he does his best to get rid of it. After the "impressive caesura", he still remains highly intelligent but learns it all again. That highly intelligent person *appears* to be very intelligent and to know and to learn easily everything that he is taught. The only trouble is that he can be extremely intelligent but not wise.

Note that I have to make a distinction between "intelligence" and "wisdom". I would hate to try to define either, but here in this group I can fall back on your assistance in grasping what I mean in spite of the inadequate articulate communication I make. You can use your own wisdom to decide for yourselves how wise you or anyone else would be to rely on the wisdom of a group. Sometimes you may find yourself in a culture which is highly intelligent but not wise; you can make up your own minds about the extent to which you would regard such a distinction illuminating in clarifying your own impressions of the group in which you find yourself. In that very activity, you add a dimension to your self; you exercise and develop your capacity for discrimination. You can rely on a certain amount of experience—possibly hearsay, possibly direct experience—which you yourself have had, to assess the nature or characteristics of the society of which we are members.

Are the inhabitants of this geographical space wiser than they were in the time of Homer, Horace or Virgil? Of course, we don't know because we cannot say what Rome was like when those poets existed. But you can have an idea whether or not *you* are wiser than you were when this meeting started. And on your answer to that question will depend whether you go on meeting together or not. That depends on daring to discriminate. How do you measure the distance between these two points—now, and the beginning of this meeting? Or the distance between Horace's Rome and today's Rome? In kilometres, hours, weeks, days? Or will somebody have to invent a system of coordinates by which we could place ourselves in mental time and space?

Those capable of mathematical thought seem to have done something about it. Euclid's geometry didn't solve the problem of parallel lines satisfactorily, but geometry, as we know it now, was *implicit* in Euclid's geometry. It took a few hundred years to become *explicit*. That depended on a growth of experience by the

Hindus with their decimal system, and Descartes with his Cartesian coordinates in which the limitations, the confines, the restrictions of Euclidean geometry could be transcended by algebraic geometry. We are no longer dependent on our eyes or even on what Milton called "inward eyes". In that way we can suppose the line that joins two points, both of which are imaginary. So I say, *dare* to use your speculative imagination, whether your culture likes it or not.

We know about the function of the adrenal glands—something which we could say is not thought at all but chemistry, biochemistry. When and how does it become possible for the individual to be able either to fight or to run away? When shall we become capable of running away from, or fighting for, the freedom to think? I have interviewed plenty of people who could not get over the fact that they had had to surrender in war and were taken prisoner. I have had good reason to mourn those who, in a hopeless situation, sacrificed their lives rather than surrender. "He who fights and runs away, lives to fight another day." But how much time have you to make up your mind? Here we can debate the problem for an hour, two hours; in real life there is not time for debate: you have to decide instantaneously whether to translate yourself into action which is apparent and clear, or whether to preserve it for another day. That is why, in producing a framework suitable for learning, there must be ample opportunity for making decisions. To put it in visual terms, one must provide a child with the space necessary for development. This applies to us also—any decision that we make, any statement that we make, should leave room for growth and development. In talking like this, I am actually producing a system, an architectonic, of my own thought. But that very fact also involves secreting a kind of calcification—I borrow the term from physiology, where we say that the arteries become hardened. We have to be aware of something similar happening with our thoughts: we become wedded to a state of mind which is serviceable, may even serve us well, and we don't want to have it disturbed. The advantage of a group of people coming together is that it is like seeing various aspects of our own personality all at the same time. Can you detect the calcification in this group? Can you detect it in yourself?

Q: I'd like to ask Dr Bion a question. Is it possible to identify any kind of relationship between the factor he has described as intelligence and wisdom and the entities he calls Ps and D?

BION: A person can often rid himself of a disturbing tendency to initiate *anything*—he prefers the depression to the state of mania. Sometimes, when the person has rid himself—at whatever stage in his life—of the unpleasant experience of constant changes from depression to jubilation, from jubilation to depression, by becoming permanently depressed or remaining in a permanent state of mania—to put it in the exaggerated form—such a person will attempt to deal with it by finding a partner who will be depressed instead of him, or who will be manic instead of him. Someone who doesn't allow himself to be too acutely observant may say, "What a happy marriage!" If you allow yourself to be more acute, you might say, "No, not a happy marriage—a *folie à deux*". There are various versions of what is basically the same thing; it depends on the extent to which you allow yourself to be sensitive to the *implicit* facts. Geometry does not change—projective algebraic geometry is implicit in Euclid's geometry and became explicit later. What is the origin of this culture? When was it implicit, and what was it implicit in? The civilization of Valerian? The civilization of Hadrian? And what civilization will be shortly occupying this space? I say "shortly" because the scale of measurement with which we are concerned is not the span of a human life—a few hundred years is nothing. What is the culture implicit in this meeting? What will it look like when it becomes explicit?

Q: Let my try to suggest some answers, or at least to reformulate some of the questions. Well, I don't know what I shall say in a little while, but I imagine I can rely on the support of the group while I speak. My feeling is that there were two simultaneous stories, at least as I experienced them. One of them had to do with me directly, as someone who was very worried in a situation of blockage, embarrassment, respect and concern, and the other was more connected with the group. One of the impressions this gave me was of a sense of rebellion stronger than my own, which I perhaps felt as a part of myself, but it also had a lot to do with our being psychoanalysts or, alternatively, with our being people meeting each other. There was something else too. On the one hand, I felt that I didn't agree with the ideas Dr Bion was putting forward about thinking, while on the other, perhaps I did.

In other words, the feeling I normally have when speaking in a group is not that I am speaking myself, but that, at the very moment when I have noticed that the group is spatialized, just as my mind is spatialized, I can speak as one of the focal points of a multidimensional conversation. On the other hand, I recognized that what Dr Bion said about the patient whose father and mother had died—had actually been murdered, leaving him alone and dependent—applied not only to me but perhaps also to other people in so far as they were not in an all-embracing group situation. Let me say just one more thing, and then I won't take up any more of your time: it's that I felt that if I had suggested creating an atmosphere—for instance, a damp atmosphere—then either I would have felt like getting drunk, having a drink together with other people, or . . . well, I'm also told that an analyst can't drink.

BION: To fall back on a physiological model: if an embolus forms in the circulatory system, it may lead to the death of the part of the body which is dependent for its supply of blood on a particular arterial system. Alternatively, a collateral circulation is formed. If this group, for example, prevented the development of thought and mental growth, then I think it would die. I have no difficulty in believing that in certain societies analysis will not survive, but there may be other societies in which a collateral circulation can be set up. Put in more general terms, I don't see any reason why the human race should survive; the function of life could be taken up by an entirely different form of animate object—like viruses, or bacteria, or bacillae. In some respects our inherited simian characteristics can be far more active and virulent than what we regard as our "human" characteristics. Our simian intelligence may be so clever at inventing tricks that it could invent an atomic bomb— only better. That would solve the problem long before we had the wisdom to know how to use our capacity for nuclear fission. At present we try to forbid the import or export of nuclear submarines and so on, but none of our statesmen would bother to prohibit the export of intelligence—and still less would they be bothered about wisdom.

We will have to have a pause for thought—I take it that our bodies have to have a certain amount of rest. So I suggest that we adjourn for our terrifying dreams or happy visions, according to taste.

Rome, 16 July 1977—Morning

Q : Last night Dr Bion asked us to express our wild thoughts and, at the same time, warned us not to express them too respectably. Then he made an interesting point about the difference between intelligence and wisdom, specifically as regards groups. I'd like to ask Dr Bion if putting one's wild thoughts into respectable form might not be equivalent to intelligence, as opposed to wisdom—in other words, a particularly well-masked form of destructiveness.

BION: It is much more difficult to reply to that question when it applies to one's own thoughts at the time. There is no way of avoiding the fundamental fact that one is always dependent and alone. When I use those words, I am using relatively highly developed articulate speech about something which is basic, fundamental and has to be experienced. Even the infant has to be able to solve that problem; it does not like the feeling of dependence or the feeling of loneliness, isolation—nor do any of us. I can practise my speculative imagination and say that the infant feels that it may express its feeling of isolation by crying, supposedly for assistance from whatever it is dependent on—the breast, the mother, the parents. Both the infant and the parent have this same problem. The child one suspects of being psychotic or borderline psychotic can be so terrified of its feelings that it expresses them by crying for help, constantly, tirelessly. But the parents do tire; their problem is whether to nurse that infant or whether to escape from the sleepless situation. So when an individual—as, for example, here—knows that he has something to say, the question is whether to say it or not, because he is afraid of discovering either that there is no one to hear or that there *is* somebody to hear but that somebody will run away. Thus the dreaded isolation is made worse, not less.

We can turn the present situation to good account by trying to decide whether to say, to express, what we have to say, or not. That may not matter very much to us here, but tomorrow the group or the culture may not be so friendly. Here you can practise expressing whatever you are capable of expressing—your distress, your happiness, your capacity—and dependent on that experience is what you express tomorrow, in much the same way as the infant's capacity to express what it feels depends on the experience that it has at its first attempt.

Practising your speculative imagination, consider this: does the infant initiate birth by trying to break out of an intolerable situation, the mother's womb or the amniotic fluid? If so, it could then feel responsible for initiating the expression of its own experience, responsible for making obvious its own existence. In today's complex situation where there is so much evidence, can we still detect vestiges, very active vestiges, of our anxiety, of our fear to express whatever it is that we are capable of? We can be afraid of expressing our stray thoughts, wherever they come from, because we are afraid of the reception they will get. And then the poet, the painter, the musician implicit in each of us does not get expressed, for fear it would be destroyed if it were.

Winnicott was once asked, "Why is the good object destroyed?" The "good object" is only a technical psychoanalytic term—I don't feel particularly impressed by the question or the problem. But I do suggest that we have a chance of seeing not *why* the good object is in danger, but that destructiveness is stimulated by the presence of something which can be destroyed. In other words, there is a primitive pleasure to be gained by the exercise of cruelty and the destruction of something which is worth destroying. In so far as we are capable of being parents, we are also vulnerable to the forces which would destroy what the creative or potentially creative parents could create. We have to become used to finding ourselves members of this particular group or culture, but we cannot get used to it unless we dare to exist in it.

Q: I thought the image with which Dr Bion began his presentation last night was very beautiful: one quite expected to see wild thoughts floating around in the room. But afterwards I wondered whether these thoughts were an emanation of the Holy Spirit, and, if not, what is Dr Bion saying? I then expected a solution to the mystery of the beginning of St John's Gospel, which would tell us where the Word was and help us to understand how it had been made flesh. But none of the rest of what was said helped me with this, and, in particular, the long discussion of man's difficult acquisition of language, starting from grunts, confused me. I felt that this beginning was contradictory: in a word, does God—or whoever—grunt, or does He speak?

Q: I thought I would tell Dr Bion that I felt the group had uttered a wild thought by bringing this previously expressed wish . . . I also thought that our discussion was, in a way, a manifestation of longing, and, provided that Dr Bion is prepared to tolerate this insistence on language, I wanted to return to the subject of music . . .

[interruption due to external noise]

BION: I can't answer that question, but you can see the answer for yourself: either I can cover my ears so I can't hear so much noise and won't have to listen to your questions, or I can get up and leave the room. In fact, with my amount of experience, I am quite capable of being deaf and blind to what I don't want to hear and see without either covering my ears or shutting my eyes. I am also capable of being geographically mobile—in fact, I shall leave Rome shortly. But I don't propose to try to take the place of your own ability; I don't propose to tell you why I leave the room, or why I am deaf and blind to what is said to me, because my answer would be prejudiced—in so far as I know it at all. You are free to use your capacity for discrimination and think what you like about my reaction. I know that it will be disappointing because I know by this time that I am only human, and I shall therefore probably do what any other human being would do. When somebody is able to make an apocalyptic statement, like the Revelations of St John, it depends on whether anybody would be prepared to hear when the individual is able to transform his thoughts and feelings into verbal expression. Milton says, "Hail, holy light . . . may I express thee unblamed?" At the end of this passage from the commencement of the third book of *Paradise Lost*, he says,

> . . . from the cheerful ways of men
> Cut off, and, for the book of knowledge fair,
> Presented with a universal blank
> Of nature's works, to me expunged and rased,
> And wisdom at one entrance quite shut out.
> So much the rather thou, Celestial Light,
> Shine inward, and the mind through all her powers
> Irradiate; there plant eyes; all mist from thence
> Purge and disperse, that I may see and tell
> Of things invisible to mortal sight.

In the Revelations, St John states it in terms of a light which is expressed verbally, but he *himself* expresses it verbally. Can we listen to that verbal expression? And can we further regard or tolerate the meaning which lies beyond the verbal expression?

In the *Baghavad Gita*, Krishna expresses doubts that Arjuna would be able to tolerate the spectacle if he were to reveal himself. In other words, it depends on the meaning which lies beyond the apocalyptic revelation. There are certain gifted people who are able to dare to express what it is that they can hear or see: "In the beginning was the Word"; "Let there be light"; "Won from the void and formless infinite."

A mathematician might try to express "infinity"; a religious person might try to express the Godhead (not God, but "the God-head"); a scientist might try to locate the source of light (Newton attempted to do so by his work on optics); Leonardo could draw a picture and say, "This is what I see"; Giotto could say, "This is what I can see." But none of them can *make* us look or listen to what is shown or said. We can be as blind, as deaf, as insensible to the composer, the painter, the dramatist who is either in ourselves or outside. Here we don't have to pay any attention to anybody—not even to ourselves or to anybody who is "not self". The advantage of coming together is that we have a chance of making our own choice. As Shakespeare puts it, "To be, or not to be, that is the question". He doesn't say what the answer is; he says, "Whether it is nobler in the mind to suffer the slings and arrows of outrageous fortune, or to take arms against a sea of troubles, and by opposing end them?" That is a choice nobody can make for the individual— except the individual. Only he can decide whether to be or not to be.

Q: We were talking about thoughts without a thinker. Let me tell you about something that I personally found very striking, which I cannot explain rationally to this day. Perhaps, in the end, it will all turn out to be much simpler than I imagine. At any rate, at about 11 o'clock on Wednesday morning I received some very sad and distressing news. On the same day, a patient began his session by saying that he felt that I was in great pain. So far, I must say I was not surprised, but then he brought a dream he had had on the Tuesday night. Putting together the dream and the associations, it was clear that they amounted to a perfect description of the event that had made me so sad. When I met Dr Bion last week, I had already been wondering whether a situation like this could be called communication.

BION: So much seems to depend on our pre-existing classifications. That is why I say that, in the actual practice of analysis, in real life— as opposed to the theories about what life is or what analysis is— you can compare the facts. Either there is something wrong with science if it does not allow room for the growth of the human spirit or mind, or we have to reconsider what we regard as "facts". What is a psychoanalyst? It appears to me that Freud aspired to a scientific standard according to his ideas of what science was at that time. I don't think that his system really made room even for his own development. After all, the quotation, "There is much more continuity between intra-uterine life and earliest infancy than the impressive caesura of birth would have us believe" [S.E. 20, p. 138], is from 1936, near the end of his life.

What happens if somebody allows himself to have an experience such as the one we have just had verbalized for us here? It seems to me that the analyst who actually participates in the experience has a chance of deciding whether to try to communicate—as he is doing here—and whether we would be capable of hearing and understanding the communication. If he is to communicate the experience, which language is he to talk? Will articulate speech do? Or would he have to be a musician, a composer, or would he have to paint it? In any case it requires courage if he is going to dare to make public, to communicate to somebody not himself, his experience. It may take a long time, either in the individual's life—which is, after all, pretty short—or in the life of the group. This sad event, this experience of sadness—where did it originate? Could it be located in some geographical place? Or could it originate in the mind of the analyst? Or could it originate in the relationship between two people? Let me take refuge in the relatively reasonable explanation and say it originates in the relationship between these two people—you can see how *rational* that would be, how in accordance with theories of transference and countertransference and so forth. But suppose we are not satisfied with that explanation. Perhaps we should then have to extend our ideas of what is science or our knowledge of the central nervous system and our capacity for receiving information via our peripheral and central nervous system. We can all be aware of the information brought to us by our "senses"—in the neurological sense—by the stimulation of our nerve endings. But the questions that have been raised here may mean that we have to become aware of the possibility that there are other receptor organs of which we are not aware. A physician, who only purports to be concerned with the body, can fall back on what his senses tell him; he can take precautions to be sensitive to the universe in which he lives. But then he also has to be able to tolerate that information and to try to understand what it means. The same thing applies to the apocalyptic vision which to some extent can be communicated to us by the greatest of our predecessors, like Leonardo, Giotto, Newton, Milton. But first of all we have to look at what they show us—and most people don't—and then, while we are looking, allow ourselves to recognize the meaning which lies beyond. It is easy to dismiss St John on the grounds that he was . . . well, one of these "queer" people. It is easy to dismiss this particular patient as a psychotic or a borderline psychotic. But what are you to do when there are two people involved—yourself and this supposedly borderline psychotic? You can hear what these two people say to each other, and you can be aware that you are not satisfied, that there is something that you do not know.

Q: When Dr Bion talks about this wild thought that is in some way waiting for us to express it, I feel that he is talking about an infantile experience, such as when a very young baby experiences the emotion of coming upon a thought of its own as a foreign body. I'd like to know his opinion on three different situations. First of all, when does each of us as an individual come into contact with his own thoughts, and how does this mating with one's own wild thought come about? Second—and this is perhaps even more interesting—how does the mating with these thoughts come about in the dyadic analytic situation?

It seems to me that in a relationship between two people, there is actually a whole crowd of characters on both sides, and so I ask myself who is thinking, why they are thinking and how these thoughts meet. There seem to be a multitude of people with wild thoughts flying back and forth all the time. But what happens in the group situation when the individual, faced with the encounter with his own thoughts, is much more alone and, in a way, much more fragmented than in the dyadic situation? In the dyadic situation of analysis, one seems to be several different people. In the group situation, what happens is like a kind of fragmentation and delegation of something of oneself to another person, to make the encounter with the wild thought less dramatic. To sum up, how is the Word made flesh in the individual, in the dyadic situation, and, on another level, in the multitude represented by the group?

BION: We come across this situation at a very late stage. We are so educated that it is practically impossible ever to get to wisdom. We can start by learning the alphabet—a, b, c ; it is stupid and it's dull.

But if we persist we may learn to put it together—c . . . a . . . t—and then somebody might say "cat" and relate it to an actual picture or animal. If this process goes on, we can learn to put words together and discover that sentences have a meaning. In that way we can reach a stage where it is almost impossible to see the words for the alphabet; and finally we cannot detect the meaning for the words. We can be so well educated that it is almost impossible to realize that life may have a meaning. Therefore, some process has to be discovered by which we could forget what we have learned in order to be sensitive to the fundamental thoughts or feelings which may still have survived—there may still be some vestige of wisdom in the human race. I don't want to adhere particularly to either an optimistic or a pessimistic position if I can avoid it, but it is difficult to remain blind to the possibility that we now know so much that we are virtually incapable of being wise. We can look at a sculpture, we can look at the written word, we can read the Revelations of St John—they can mean nothing if we are so clever that we cannot see the meaning of what is pointed out to us. I don't see any alternative to allowing ourselves to practise, as opposed to theorize; to live instead of theorizing about living. Victor Hugo suggests that the physical world of which we are aware is, indeed, the creation of some God or Spirit. Another of these gifted people said, "The heavens declare the glory of God: and the firmament sheweth his handy-work" [Psalm 19]. Even astronomers are trying to read—not books, but the heavens themselves. Someone else could be engaged in examining this same universe through a microscope. So the group as a whole has a wide view—we can examine this universe in which we find ourselves with a microscope, or a 200-inch reflector, or a radio-telescope. Between the lot of us we might make some small contribution in much the same way as somebody has contributed to who or what we are today.

At some point, before birth, we can feel, fairly rationally, that we are individuals inside another individual. What the communication is between the environment of the mother's womb and the infant, depends on some sort of contact between the two—whether it be physical or something else. Is the embryo, at the stage of three somites, when the optic and auditory pits are beginning to form, capable of receiving some sort of impression? When is the mother aware of having a character or a person inside her? At a comparatively late stage of pregnancy, I think a mother is aware of the athletic feats of this object inside. Is it something which is going to grow into a violent creature which will attack the body from outside? Or will it turn into a ballet dancer?

These questions can be stimulated now, after this meeting, tomorrow, and so on as long as we exist. We can attempt to read the writings, the monuments which have been bequeathed to us, but there is also the problem of reading the universe which impinges upon us *now* and in which—as I have said—we might just as well be embryos in contact with a gaseous environment. If you are capable of painting, the sooner you learn it the better. If you are capable of composing a musical vocabulary, musical words and sentences, it would be useful to know that. If you are a writer, the sooner you learn a vocabulary and how to use it the better. It is no good learning *my* vocabulary—that might be useful as a transitory phase, a point at which you lodged on the way to discovering your own vocabulary and how to use it. That is why my answers to these questions are of no consequence. That is simply knowledge which then acts as an obstruction to your own discoveries. Similarly, it is quite useful to know what this culture is, but not if the culture takes the place of where you are. The space which you occupy cannot be occupied by somebody else without sacrifice of yourself.

Q: This comment is directed more to the other people in the group than to Dr Bion. It seems to me that Dr Bion is suggesting not that we should perfect our learning, but, perhaps, that we should partake of a creative moment, rather like partaking of Raphael's creativity when he contemplated the Mona Lisa (sorry!). The Mona Lisa will never give us an answer to the problems of our personal existence, let alone our scientific existence, and yet I think that by reflecting on the ambiguity of the Mona Lisa, we might be in a slightly better position to accept our personal difficulties and see them in a clearer light. Our setting in this seminar is perhaps ambiguous because we have probably all read Bion and learnt how much attention he pays to questions.

It is my mistake if I come here expecting Bion to be able to answer the questions he has raised in his books. Perhaps the truth of the matter is that, in this personal contact with Dr Bion, we see only the confirmation that acceptance of the questioning within ourselves is the only way to stimulate the very painful process represented by our personal creativity.

BION: I think it is what psychoanalysts are trying to express when they talk about a "transference relationship"—that is to say, that we have these preconceptions that there is some sort of authority, a father or a mother, who knows the answer. The aim in analysis is to make that point clear, not so that you can go on feeling how important that person is for the rest of your existence, but because you can then discard it and make room for whatever ideas you might want to express yourself. In the meantime, the analyst can appear to occupy a more and more important position, but it should only be a temporary affair drawing attention to the fact that the analyst is supposed to know this, that or the other thing, just like a father or a mother. The importance of the analyst's position is brought to light so that it can be discarded; the supposed authority becomes redundant, the position of the analyst is no longer useful. This is why it is important to learn, if you can, during the transition stage who the musician, the painter, the poet is who is struggling to get free from inside you.

Rightly or wrongly we behave as if we thought there was such a thing as a mind, a character, a spirit. There are a number of inadequate descriptions—soul, spirit, supersoul, ego, superego, id. They are not very illuminating. But when, in your ordinary life or in your consulting-room, you come across another "something", like the patient who appeared to dream the fact of sadness, then how will you clothe that discovery in words, and what words will you clothe it in?

Rome, 16 July 1977—Afternoon

B ION: Does anyone feel the urge to express an idea or have an idea expressed?

Q: I'd like to ask something: against the background of informal thinking of the last few days, and influenced by what Dr Bion has said at our meetings over the past week, the question of a concept of time occurred to me several times. The way things emerge in the present had seemed to me to be a peculiarity of the group situation, but it also came up, for me, in a dyadic setting— not only as a trick of the trade, but as the only possible way to relate or, rather, to exist. Well, how does Dr Bion see time? Is it a property of space? Is it the act of linking or the conscious link between two or more spaces? Is it the way we perceive our mental space as alive and filled with living objects? . . . How are we to ensure that the concept of relativity that follows from the abolition of definitions does not coincide with stasis?

BION: It would be interesting to know what has stimulated or caused this particular topic to be initiated. As it has been initiated *here*, it may be possible to form an idea about the source from which this problem has been derived. We can hear the actual person who has asked that question, so we can locate among all of us individuals the particular geographical spot at which this idea of "time" has emerged. We can also feel that we would like to be able to locate the space from which it originated—it would appear to be at a particular spot, which we could describe by giving the name of the person asking the question or by observing whereabouts in the room it seemed to arise. So far, it lies within the capacity of our senses; we can use our eyes and our sense of hearing; and we can use both the binaural capacity and the binocular capacity to see the point of intersection. Suppose—or, in other words, imagine, use your speculative imagination—that this group has a character. Going on from there and making a further supposition, a further speculation, could the fact that that sort of thought or idea was given expression be regarded as evidence for the existence of the mind or character of the group? Could we compare it with another collection of people? Would they also give evidence of being concerned with this question of time and space? It seems to me that they would, because if I look at today's newspaper, I see a date mentioned on it; it is stated there that in someone's opinion—and it isn't usually disputed—we occupy a particular point in time. If we look at the paper we may also get evidence that someone believes that this is a particular geographical space: if we examine the stone monuments, we get what appears to be evidence that there used to be groups that also thought so at a different time from the present one. So there does seem to be evidence—at least to me—for the existence of a human mind. I wonder if a scientist would be convinced that this was evidence of the existence of a human mind; I could ask him what evidence he had for supposing that there was such a thing as civilized or group behaviour, but it depends on what we consider to be "evidence". We are familiar with people who regard psychoanalysts as being wildly astray in their various theories, hypotheses, but I would like to know what the physical scientist's criterion is and how he considers what *he* regards as evidence for facts as in any way different from what I, for want of anything better, regard as facts myself.

If we watch a group of young children, we see signs of the kind of thing *I* might have thought when I was their age. I can suppose that there was a time when I noticed that things which presented themselves to my senses were not within my reach and I would therefore have to resort to some sort of locomotion to get to them. That would give rise to a feeling which might grow into an idea later, that there was such a thing as time and space which divided me from the object which presented itself to my senses. I could hope to be reminded of almost any state of mind of which I was at some time conscious, and I could use such knowledge or experience as I have to re-assess that evidence for time and space. How much more validity would I be justified in attaching to the evidence for which I depend on this wristwatch—a bit of modern machinery—or how much more value would I attach to a thing which I can see with the aid of a microscope, or a radio-telescope, or anything between the two? Am I to evaluate my present idea about time and space vis-à-vis the idea of time and space that I would have if I were a hungry baby trying to get at what I regarded as some desirable sweet from which I was separated? *"Le silence éternel de ces espaces infinis m'effraie"* [Pascal, *Pensées*]. I couldn't say that if I were a baby, but I could *feel* it; I could feel that it would be a terrible thing if I had to find the time and the athletic ability to get from here to there. In the meantime, I would be starved for the sensuous satisfaction which I craved to achieve.

If we have minds and need to satisfy our curiosity, we have to find a mode or a scale of measurement. I wonder if that has anything whatever to do with reality, or whether it has much more to do with the ineffectual nature of ourselves. For example, I have read that the distance across the nebula of which the sun is a part, measured through the galactic centre, is estimated as 10^8 million light-years; the space we occupy at the present time, in absolute space, we shall reoccupy again in 10^8 million light-years. I don't know whether anybody here feels any the wiser—I don't. But it sounds terribly knowing and terribly wise. As far as I am concerned it means virtually nothing, except that somebody is feeling better.

On the whole, we fall back on something simpler: we say we meet at four o'clock today, or at a quarter past nine tonight. That will do for our infantile capacity to do a bit of mental crawling.

Q: Between omnipotence and impotence, between dependence and being alone, there are thoughts about power which I don't know how to think.

BION: That again brings the problem into an area in which it seems we are able to work effectively. That is to say, if we discover that we do not know how to think—although apparently we have the apparatus which might make it possible—then at least we can try to learn how to use such capacity for thought as we *do* have. That still supposes that we have a capacity for thought, that we have a brain, or a CNS, or a sympathetic system which somehow enables us to think. If the supposition were correct, it would be necessary to learn how to use this newly discovered capacity. At present, I think the vast majority of us simply assume that *of course* we can think. And what *I* believe to be thoughts, other people may consider to be nonsense—which is a simple solution of the problem. But when we discover that we do *not* know how to think, although we are apparently able to use our CNS and the senses which this makes available to us, the question is, do we know the meaning of what our senses tell us? We assume that we understand the meaning which our senses give us; we do seem to meet together here by using our senses—that is, by being aware of what the information is that they bring us and also understanding the meaning of that information. It is not a particularly profound discovery, but we may have our ambitions stimulated to do a bit more than that. There is something to be said for the idea that if we can cooperate, if we can get so far as to come into the same room at the same time, then perhaps we can collaborate enough to achieve something more than that. We might debate this matter which has been initiated by somebody asking about time and space. And then, if we can collaborate further, we may, by our combined knowledge, make more inroads into our ignorance.

Q: I have a question. One of the pillars of Freud's work is the reality principle, which is also one of the fundamental parameters for assessing analytic work. It also seems to me that most of us, when we refer to reality so as to measure, evaluate and assess it, are as a rule referring to a whole series of spatio-temporal parameters. I also feel that one of the foundations of Bion's thought and work is the reference to truth, so I wonder what use can be made of these spatio-temporal parameters. I'm not saying that there is no reference in Freud to the problem of truth—for example, he mentions it explicitly towards the end of the Schreber case, where he asks whether there is more truth in the scientific mode of expression or in Schreber's way. I myself wonder if there are parameters or coordinates that can help us to feel that we are dealing with truth (beyond the effects—for example, feeling better or feeling worse . . .).

BION: I think we should resist the temptation, the seduction to believe in our own omnipotence and omniscience. There is plenty of evidence to bring it home to us that we are neither omnipotent nor omniscient—we are not even successful in doing the simplest things. Our reaction to the discovery, so constantly repeated, that we are not omnipotent or omniscient is nearly always to swing over in the opposite direction; the belief in our omnipotence and omniscience is directly built on the foundation of our knowledge that we are ignorant and incompetent. Let me say the same thing in what may appear to be a different way: our feelings of helplessness, ignorance, incapacity are brought home to us because they are based on the foundation of our omnipotence and omniscience. The more we think we are omnipotent and omniscient, the more certain it is that it is brought home to us that we are nothing of the sort; so we oscillate between one and the other—we are constantly making that journey between A and B.

That might point in the direction of establishing some absolute value in the way that mathematicians do. But this comes nearer to having to invent or create the tools with which to think. While you are attempting to analyse the mind of somebody who is not you, or the relationship between the two minds, you also have to invent or create the very tools you hope to use. Here, we can watch and listen to us trying to learn how to think. That particular space and that particular silence are so penetrating that we get frightened of them. To repeat the quotation from Pascal, "*Le silence éternel de ces espaces infinis m'effraie*"; we are frightened of the penetrating quality of silence. It is not only a matter of being afraid of what we say and think and make audible; it is also fear of what we do *not* say. The musicians have a way of actively symbolizing this with things which they call "rests"; they can record the "rest" as part and parcel of the music. If the orchestra is really in contact with the reality to which it can give expression, then sometimes the coop- eration between the various instrumentalists and the conductor will feel different from what it does on other occasions when they are playing the same piece of music. You can say that the orchestra gave a very fine performance of, say, Brahms's Fourth Symphony. What piece of music are we expressing here—"The Collected Works of Freud"? "The History of Philosophy"? "The History of Religion"? We talk about being "psychiatrists" and "psychoanalysts". Are we? Or shall we become so one day?

Wordsworth says, ". . . hearing often-times the still, sad music of humanity" ["Lines Composed a Few Miles Above Tintern Abbey"]. We are supposed to be in contact with our fellow human beings. When you give an interpretation tomorrow, are you sure that it will approximate to expressing the music of humanity or the little bit of it which has got into your consulting-room?

Note that there I have introduced an element of rhythm, timing. Most of us probably have the experience of sometimes feeling that "that was a good session", when we were really together with one of our patients. We were acting in conformity with a rhythm, even if we couldn't describe it or record it.

Q: Let me suggest something. If we consider the etymology, *pensare* [the Italian for "thinking"] means taking on a weight, *pondus*; the same is true of pondering, in the sense of weighing up—they are all synonymous. *Cogitare*, on the other hand, is interactive with *cogere*, which means "to constrain". So I wonder if a concept of mass and gravity could be introduced into the theory of thought. Thinking would then be tantamount to being compelled to support or lift weights. In that case, one could imagine a kind of gravity applicable to thought, too, which warps its space. My question is this: can we say, "Give me a fulcrum, give me a sign of support, and I will lift up a thought for you"? Also, is the group generally an instrument that is more capable or less capable of acting as a lever for lifting up thoughts?

BION: The metaphorical use you mention shows that at some time human beings have been aware of this "weight". It crops up now because this use has not been good enough; the question then is whether the group could refine the capacity for thought which has so far been achieved. "*Mene, mene, tekel, upharsin*" [Daniel 5:25]—

that was a definite resort to a language which we ordinarily use for describing quantity or weight. The problem today is, are you able to be sufficiently sensitive, either here or in your consulting-room or in your home, to be able to hear the mention of these weights and measures? Could you then consider what they were measuring in that state of mind? If so, then perhaps we could add a dimension to our capacity to think. We may not make much progress, but the fact that we are thinking may strengthen our mental musculature. Could this group think and talk and discuss in such a way that our mental capacity would be able to carry a bigger load at the end of an hour, a day, a week, than it could at the beginning?

Q: I'd like to add something to what the previous questioner said, about whether there can be a fulcrum on which to rest thought. There are two things here. The first is whether this fulcrum can be thought of in relation to the group's ethical, rather than its aesthetic, reference. The second point is completely separate: it concerns Leonardo da Vinci's idea of weight, which I can't remember in detail but will quote in part. It goes something like this: "The lover moves towards the loved object like sense towards the sensible . . ." I don't recall the whole quotation, but at one point he says: "if the loved object is base, the lover becomes base, and if the loved object is good, it gives satisfaction and gratification." Then there is a reference to weight: "So the lover rests and the object settles there"—which I would like to put together with the idea of resting on something. I apologize, because it's a while since I read this quotation. I wondered if this resting, the possibility of putting one's weight on something, might be a reaction, in a group situation, to what we can imagine as the ethical reference—that is, the possibility of respecting other people's thought. The example that occurred to me this morning was Freud's essay on Leonardo da Vinci, where he puts forward a number of hypotheses about Leonardo, respecting his thought on the aesthetic level without doing violence to it. I'd like to know Dr Bion's opinion.

Bion: Leonardo was one of these people who appears to have had a very great mind, a very great personality; indeed, the remains he left still have a powerful effect on people who are living long after his death. Horace was another inhabitant who is supposed to have lived geographically in this area. His "Ode to Pyrrha" has worried a great many people: in it he describes the painful consequences of having fallen in love with Pyrrha's golden hair. In navigating that particular sea, he appears to have come to shipwreck and has hung his dripping clothes as a memorial to the experience. I find it very moving to see portrayed on the walls of an Etruscan tomb the costume presumably worn by the inhabitant. That is a pictorial representation of what looks remarkably like a similar state of mind: it seems to be expressing a similar difficulty with regard to the passion of love. Clearly there seems to be something which brings two different human beings together; whatever the outcome of their coming together, whether it is shipwreck or continued journey, it appears to be a very stimulating experience. So those who are disposed to launch themselves on the stormy seas of love are risking a painful and frightening experience of shipwreck. Our problem here involves not only being able to think intellectually, but also being able to feel emotionally. Let me put the question again: what wild thoughts and what wild feelings are you prepared to risk giving a home to?

Q: I've been nurturing a wild thought for about three-quarters of an hour now. I need to tell the story of a film I thought of when Dr Bion talked about omniscience, omnipotence and leaving space. Its title is *Phase IV*, and it's a science-fiction film. The plot is about two scientists, an ethologist and a doctor, who are assigned to investigate an invasion of ants somewhere in America. On arrival, they find totems, monuments built by the ants. Nearby, they build a "biodome". The ethologist bombs the monuments to smithereens, causing the ants to run amok. The men try to destroy the ants with a yellow acid. The surviving ants take away this yellow material a little at a time. Then these yellow ants surround the dome and build pyramids, or pyra- mid-like parallelepipeds—set up so as to reflect the sun's light on to the dome. At this point a very important new element is introduced into the story: a girl survivor of the yellow acid joins the scientists in the dome. The ethologist who was studying the ants *in vitro* is bitten by them, and the girl has a fit of hysterics and breaks the test-tubes. The ethologist is intent on destroying the ants, so he goes outside to smash the pyramids that focus the sun's heat on the dome and raise its temperature. But the cybernetician manages to establish a human relationship with the girl and, to make contact, makes a square for the ants—in other words, he tries to use this square as a language. The ants respond with a circle, with another smaller circle inside it. At this point the girl feels the need, or possibly the wish, to sacrifice herself—in other words, she thinks the ants want *her*. So she goes outside. As for the ethologist, he has been driven completely mad by the ant bites and, leaving the dome, is killed by the ants. The cybernetician is very disturbed by all this and goes to look for the queen: he goes down a tapering tunnel in the hope of finding her there. Instead of the queen, a hand appears, and then the girl. Then the film cuts to a different scene.

It ends with a man and a woman walking in the hills, which have been transformed by the ants—I don't know what happens then; perhaps they'll make another film.

BION: What strikes me about this is that I cannot imagine how the adrenals could ever get a mode of expression, although I can see that through a relatively short space of time, a few hundred years, vestiges of their activity could emerge in the human mind. And then at last the poor inarticulate glandular substances could find expression, aided by the machinery of film, film projectors and mass advertisement. So we get a modern representation of flight and fight which, with the combined wisdom of the human race, can produce a modern method of dispersal of the message which the adrenals presumably could never have expressed. In this way it might also be possible to add a little quota to the whole by drawing attention to speculative imagination and speculative reason, elaborating a continuation of the conflict between the capacities for flight, fight and dependence. So far, the human animal has been pretty good at destroying its rivals. But every now and then, it is not so successful: in 1918 there was an outbreak of influenza, or Spanish 'flu, or "pyrexia of unknown origin"—PUO. In a short space of a few weeks those minute objects—viruses—killed off even more human beings than human beings had managed to destroy in the war. Our capacity for self-destruction hardly requires augmentation; there are plenty of forces waiting to do the job and to put an end to such creative capacities as we have. Perhaps somebody would like to write the script for a film of a war between the adrenals and the gonads. Perhaps we should end by all being impotent or infertile, or perhaps make the world uninhabitable because there were too many of us. I shall wait—though I may not last long enough—to hear the continuation of that film. Perhaps it won't be just a film; perhaps at this present time we ought to prepare our minds and capacities for future dangers to which our present and past ones are just the hors-d'oeuvre. The capacity for thought needs to be fostered so that it becomes much more capable and much more robust than it is. Even our ability here to debate is easily affected by the sight of a helicopter over the building, a dog barking, or motor traffic. An ability to think and debate which is as vulnerable as that is just not good enough. As a by-product of the discussion, we hope for a stronger, more robust and more accurate method of thought.

At this point the time that we heard about earlier in the meeting dictates to us again that we have to disperse.

Rome, 16 July 1977—Evening

Freud was impressed by certain caesuras, but they are, in fact, multitudinous. Birth and death both seem to create a mental turbulence; it is possible that we ourselves notice the up-heaval when we are born and change from a watery fluid to a gaseous fluid, from the amniotic fluid to air. But it is the birth of someone else which creates the disturbance in the already existing people—usually the mother and father. Death also creates a distur-bance in the survivors. But that doesn't mean that birth or death are of any importance as far as the individual is concerned. We can easily imagine that if we fail to be born adequately that would create a disturbance; similarly if we fail to be adequately killed, or fail to die.

When I was studying medicine I became familiar with the saying, "Do not strive officiously to keep alive", meaning "Don't go out of your way to keep somebody alive, officiously". Thanks to the scientists it is now possible to keep certain bodily functions operat-ing—for whose benefit I don't know. Recently there was a notori-ous case in which the parents were extremely anxious that all this apparatus should be allowed to cease functioning so that the pa-tient, their daughter, could die. Their wish was disregarded. The

antivivisectionists used to object to animal nerve-muscle prepara-
tions which were used in the teaching of students in physiology.
The case to which I refer was one in which the human being was
used like a nerve-muscle preparation. Cui bono? To whose benefit
is it?

To get back to these periods which seem to create a powerful
impression on living people: babies are born, and people die. Once
we are alive, we can die at any time. So how many funerals are we
going to celebrate? How many deaths are we going to exalt into
ritualistic upheavals? Each one of us who exists at the beginning of
a meeting, like this, has ceased to exist almost every second of time
that passes from then onwards; we have all changed into different
people. What we were before that is not important; it rapidly
becomes the past about which we can do nothing.

As I say, periods or episodes like birth, adolescence, latency,
marriage, death seem to release an emotional turmoil, so a great
deal of importance is attributed to these caesuras whenever they
appear to obtrude into our notice. The emotional turbulence which
is initiated is of some consequence because all sorts of elements, to
which we don't usually pay much attention and of which we are
not aware, get churned up and thrown onto the surface. They are
often so noticeable that we give them a name—I tried to summarize
it in a talk called "Break Up, Break Down, Break Through". I could
almost say, "Choose Your Own Preposition". But we as analysts
should use these words carefully; if we are going to talk about
"break down" or "break up", at least let us be clear in our own
minds by which coordinate system we are measuring the direction
of the break. You need to make your own vocabulary and to be
quite clear what *you* mean when you use a particular word, so that
you always use it consistently. Pressure is put on us when people
who are not used to speaking with care say, "So-and-So is having a
breakdown." I don't think you should be seduced into the belief
that the person concerned is having a breakdown—a break, yes,
but leave yourself a chance to come to your own conclusion about
the direction in which that break is occurring. Socially we don't
need to argue the point; we can agree and fall in with the ordinary
everyday use of language. But we shouldn't allow that to blunt the
language that each one of us uses. It is possible, of course, in a
group like this, that we might elaborate a common language which

could be understood by all of us, but the essential thing is your own private language which has to be kept in good working order.

Q: An essay on truth and falsehood begins with a metaphor taken from Hans Christian Andersen's tale "The Nightingale". It goes more or less like this. A forest extended from the boundary of the Emperor of China's gardens to the sea. Sailors told of a nightingale singing in a tree in the forest. The emperor wanted to have this nightingale for himself at all costs and threatened his inept courtiers with death and destruction if they failed to bring it to him. In the end, a lowly kitchen-maid was able to help the searchers; the Emperor had the nightingale, which made him happy, and the nightingale felt rewarded by the Emperor's delight. Seven sons of seven samurai were given his name. But the Emperor of Japan, who was envious, one day sent a gift of a mechanical nightingale to the Emperor of China. Its song seemed more beautiful than the real nightingale's. A music-master wrote seven theoretical volumes about the song of the mechanical nightingale. The real nightingale flew away in a huff. The mechanical nightingale unfortunately broke down, and the Emperor lay dying, from the pain of the loss of his music. The courtiers had given him up for dead, but that night the real nightingale came back to the Emperor, remembering how moved he had been in the past. Entering the Emperor's bedroom, the courtiers were astonished not to find him dead. He was standing up and happily bade them good morning. I won't report what the story says but, instead, my conclusion. After these seminars, I felt I understood that the truth might be displaced from the nightingale and found in the Emperor's suffering. Or perhaps in the suffering of the two Emperors. But I'd like to ask Dr Bion if a different vertex can be detected in this story—something about the truth that can rescue the situation. I'd been thinking about life.

BION: One of the peculiarities of certain forms of communication is that they are hieroglyphic, pictorial—Chinese, for example. The objection to that method of communication is usually that it is somewhat clumsy and ambiguous. Indeed, according to Fenollosa, the number of characters which are used in Chinese hieroglyphic writing can be reduced enormously; it is said that only about four thousand are really necessary; the remainder, which certainly amount to at least ten thousand, are redundant. Take this particular fable: it must have taken quite a long time to transform it into present-day articulate European languages; the hieroglyph has to be changed into a verbal version of a pictorial image. For our purposes, in our vocabulary, I think it is necessary to cut down the characters to a minimum; the same thing with regard to the pictorial images which we have to use. What store of verbal images and articulate words belonging to an articulate language are we to keep to draw on? And how is that vocabulary to be integrated in order to express something which we want someone not ourselves to understand? In this group it would be a great advantage if we had a common language. You can see what a nuisance it is when somebody like myself comes into the group and cannot talk a language which you all understand: it is a nuisance to you, and it is a nuisance to me.

Q: I'd like to say something—that is, I'd like to try to express this idea: what I have understood is that we need to try to listen. And also to see with our senses and . . . I'll stop there. Even though I feel that this causes tiredness and danger.

Q: . . . I felt from the beginning that deciding whether or not to express my thoughts did not matter very much, because I felt encouraged mainly to recover my capacity for internal listening—possibly by dropping my guard. But when I decided to express my thought, I felt anxious about the dependence and loneliness that could arise if someone were to listen to me and then go away. But the anxiety of loneliness and dependence could become intolerable if my internal listener also went away.

BION: I am not sure what you feel is the problem there. Is there any reason for supposing it would go away?

Q: The internal listener might go away together with the external listener.

BION: But if you know that, what is the difficulty?

Q: It might make it harder to express anxiety, to express my own thoughts, and increase the tendency to listen to them only inside myself.

BION: The feeling of being dependent *and* alone is fundamental; it seems to antedate any ability to employ articulate or any other form of speech between two people. The first person with whom we have to be able to communicate, the most important person in this context, is yourself.

I used to try to deal with that sort of situation by writing or recording notes. Nowadays I don't bother. I don't know what I am going to say in response to the emotional situation in which I find myself here. Experience teaches me that I am sure to be dissatisfied with what I say, but it also teaches me that I have to put up with the fact that I am me and that, whether I like it or not, I have to tolerate my own way of talking and thinking. Here, I am dependent on having what I say translated into a more comprehensible language. But this happens in any case; when I wish to communicate what I think to someone who is not me, then I have to use a language which, as near as I can make out, will be understood by the person to whom I address myself. I have to put up with the fact that I may not remember what I said in the previous session, or last week, or last year. On the whole I am persuaded that what I say and think has a certain coherence. I don't know what the coherence is, but I have to be reconciled to that.

Q: What is the place—the *topos*—where the individual and himself meet? The individual and the other, the individual and the group? Might it be the place where thought and action, spirit and matter, come together?

BION: I am not particularly illuminated by the various descriptions of the mind or personality—ego, id, superego, and so forth. A Jesuit I know of speaks of the "arbitrium", a name he gives to a function which acts as a final judge. I am not convinced by giving any particular name to the fact that I seem to discriminate and choose to say one thing and not to say the other. I think there is every reason to treat our verbal communications as an action which is similar to athletic action. I see no evidence for giving it a name.

Nor would I agree with people who somewhat contemptuously dismiss the whole of psychoanalysis and philosophy as "so much talk".

Tacitus describes how the Germanic tribes used a method by which a bard expressed himself, and in accordance with the reaction of the group to that aesthetic communication, the leader decided what impulses were to be translated into physical activity like going to war. There are also legends about the songs the sirens sang. Perhaps each of us may be able to make some contribution to this problem of "what is it?" or "who is it?" who decides in the republic of our own personalities which thought or action is to be translated into further action.

Walter Landor puts it in this way;

There are no fields of amaranth on this side of the grave.
There are no voices . . . that are not soon mute, however tuneful.
There is no name with whatever emphasis of passionate love
    repeated
Of which the echo is not faint at last.

[Walter Savage Landor, *Imaginary Conversations*]

Each of us, so long as we live, appears to be able to record various experiences in the course of his lifetime. Something seems to be able to determine what, out of all that store, is worthy of recall. But there is still the problem of deciding what to do with it. We may be able to come to some kind of temporary conclusion as to how we are to decide. It is complex: a number of thoughts, ideas, feelings are stirred up, and almost instantaneously we put them into an order of precedence. That is very much of an intellectualization, and I am not particularly satisfied that it is a fair representation of the facts.

Q: In all these seminars we have touched upon the subject of death, and I believe that, if what we have said is to be coherent and efficacious, we need to be able to encounter the Buddha—and also to be able to kill him. I'd like to ask Dr Bion if he thinks that the discussion we are having at this moment has any connection with Freud's reflections in the short paper where he is accompanied by a poet ["On Transience", *S.E.* 14]: together they see a field of flowers and reflect that although they will die, it is nevertheless worth while to live and work.

Q: I, too, would like to ask something. When you spoke about the listener and establishing a language of one's own, does this have to do with bringing about a situation where, when we say something in the course of analysis, we say it first of all to ourselves, and can this give rise to growth?

BION: I am not sufficiently acquainted with the *Upanishads* to be familiar with the earlier formulations about the human mind and the human spirit. There are certainly some works which appear to establish a contact with Western modes of thinking. The *Baghavad Gita* is one of them; there is a distorted version, by Fitzgerald, of *Omar Khayyam*; there is a French version of *The Iliad* which is said to be the best there is. There is a curious similarity between various races and times—for example, the prophet who is supposed to be able to voice the opinions of God. Moses, Jesus, Mohammed are all said to have expressed the will and views of God. The Muslims seem to regard the Hebrews as having gone astray, and to have done so markedly on the occasion when Moses descended from Sinai and found them worshipping the golden calf. The Christians likewise, according to Mohammed, have made the mistake of deserting to a polytheistic religion by not being faithful to a monotheistic one. Although the subsidiary gods are, as it were, clothed in the characteristics of sainthood, it is a return to polytheism and a departure from monotheism—the vital and essential part of the religious outlook. Accordingly, the Muslims regard both the Hebraic and the Christian religions as having departed from the true religion. What about the psychoanalytic sainthood? Do you detect any signs, in the mental sphere, of stratification? Kleinianism? Freudianism? And in what direction would you say these strata are discernible? Is it possible to detect in our debate here any signs of what I call "stratification"? Geologically, of course, we can see these strata—sometimes they are up-ended like pillars; sometimes they lie horizontally. We can imagine that in a time of upheaval the strata become bent in all directions; the various religions and patron saints are fragmented and can only be described as being in a state of turbulence, of constant movement. And then it gives way to a period of relative quiescence and apparent security. But the strata still remain and can still be detected—these multitudinous gods, together with their followers.

Pressure is frequently put on an individual to suppose that he or she is one of these important people. It is very misleading—there are fashions in these religious attitudes. The god who is thrown up and exalted, rapidly disappears. Remember the poem,

"My name is Ozymandias, king of kings;
Look on my works, ye Mighty, and despair!"
Nothing beside remains. Round the decay
Of that colossal wreck, boundless and bare
The lone and level sands stretch far away.

[Shelley, *Ozymandias*]

I don't think we should be too depressed if we can see these stratifications appearing, or, to change the metaphor from geology to religion, these varieties of polytheism. We can regard them as temporary, transient phases in our journey.

Q: May I ask Dr Bion what he thinks of the daily organization of one's own mind, and whether it can facilitate dialogue with one's internal interlocutor.

Bion: I think it is dangerous to assume that we are in any way exempted from the general movement in a community. Freud described a situation in which the mere change of the observer is liable to be mistaken for a new discovery in psychoanalysis, or a new form of psychoanalysis. I mentioned before the point about modern geometry being implicit in Euclidean geometry; at some time it became explicit—it seems to be almost accidental, as if, for example, the Cartesian coordinates were a by-product off the main line of Descartes' thought, and yet very important.

Q: I wanted to say that this evening I'm constantly thinking of a poem. It describes the act of finding names for things. The poet seems very pleased, very happy, that he has this capability. At the end of the poem, he imagines he can see a beautiful ring at the bottom of a lake of particularly clear water. He also realizes that he is absolutely unable to think of a name for this object. But this seems only to increase his joy. So I'd like to ask Dr Bion if he thinks that this difficulty in naming—like the particular difficulty we sometimes have in making the implicit explicit—might perhaps be added to the series of caesuras we have been talking about . . .

BION: It could be a caesura which impressed him, and he may be able to communicate that experience verbally to you and to others because of his capacity as a poet.

I think we are all liable, in accordance with our individual natures, to be impressed by some particular caesura which may not mean very much to other people. One of these impressive things is what we might call "cure". There is a tendency for the group to pursue the shadow of a caesura; we pursue a particular relic or idea as if it really existed. In psychoanalysis there is an implicit idea that if we go through that discipline we shall achieve a cure. I see a certain difficulty: there is one particular capacity which I have come across over and over again—so much so that I would regard anyone as being extremely deficient if he couldn't make a fool of his analyst. A patient who couldn't make a fool of me must indeed have something wrong with him. It is difficult to tolerate: consider what you would feel about a person who succeeds in making a fool of you. Nevertheless, anybody who aspires to helping his suffering fellow men and women has to be sufficiently robust to survive being made a fool of.

When I happened to get swept into hospital in England, I saw the elaborate laboratory tests and auxiliary forces of nurses and hospital wards used to cure diabetics. These people were having extended to them the resources of the Welfare State. Part of it consisted in being allowed to be visited by their friends and relations. So, on the one hand, there was extended to them the diet in accordance with the findings of medical science about dietetics: on the other hand, their friends and relatives, taking pity on these poor people whose freedom was being restricted by the cruel hospital doctors and nurses, would see to it that they were plentifully supplied with the kind of food that they really liked. I didn't stay there long enough to see what was the outcome of that particular story, but when we are proposing the correct—in our view—

mental nourishment, we also have to be aware of the fact that there are plenty of other people who will supply what *they* consider to be the correct mental nourishment. You will probably soon come across a professional paper depicting the need to reassure and comfort terminally ill patients by telling them something to act as an antidote to their belief that they are dying. I wonder what chance advocating the truth would have against forces of that nature.

Rome, 17 July 1977

We are all concerned with mental health from a responsible position. I am not considering as a part of our immediate discussion what we as individuals feel; as people in a position of responsibility with regard to patients, what we feel mentally or physically is a matter of no consequence whatsoever. It matters to us individually, but to no one else. It doesn't matter how tired we are, how physically or mentally ill—all those are matters of complete indifference. They are only *facts*, like any other facts about which we can do nothing and about which nobody else is going to do anything either. Your mental or physical health is a fact like the weather or the geographical location in which you are working, which is otherwise of no consequence. Whatever those facts may be, as responsible people we have to exercise our skill; we have to be capable of thinking clearly, no matter what is going on.

Our problem is how to be sensitive to the sufferings of people who come to us for assistance, but not to be so affected by them as to interfere with our thinking clearly about the work in hand. In certain situations we can be unmistakably aware of the danger in which we are, particularly those in which we are threatened with physical violence. It is still important that we should continue to think clearly even when it is also clear that our lives are in danger. But most of the time, that sort of danger is not at all obvious; our circumstances can appear to be comfortable and consequently reassuring.

In war, most of the people who are engaged in the combatant forces are aware that the fact that there are medical services is really irrelevant. It could be very seductive; it might seem to exert such a pressure that troops would like to be looked after instead of having to fight the enemy. Even in putting forward that picture I am drawing attention to something which is relatively simple. It is difficult to realize that analysts and those concerned with helping mental sufferers face any dangers. In the mental sphere one point can become clear: we find ourselves alone in a room with a particularly violent patient; there is not much we can do about it because most of us haven't the muscular, physical strength to cope with such a patient. It *is* possible to be prepared to use such physical capacity as we have. For example, if your room is high up, then it is obvious that the patient could resort to throwing himself—or the analyst, of course—out of the window. Therefore, during the time that you are seeing that patient, place yourself between him and the window. It would, in fact, be preferable not to have the consulting-room in such a position that it would be easy for the patient to commit suicide or murder by using the distance between the room and the earth below.

I found this a somewhat alarming and yet stimulating fact when I was director of the London Clinic of Psycho-Analysis, where there were no lifts and *all* our patients had to climb to the top of the house to be seen for analytic purposes. I cannot remember now how many stairs they had to climb to get to the consulting-rooms—and therefore how many stairs there were available for throwing themselves down with disastrous consequences. So we took various palliative steps which were supposed to act as an antidote to the situation in which we found ourselves. I don't know who felt better as a result of those steps, but I am reminded of the statement made by a famous British commander-in-chief, Wellington, when reviewing his troops: "I don't know what effect my troops will have on the enemy, but they certainly terrify me."

The best and the most highly qualified collaborator we have in analysis is the patient; the outcome of the meeting depends on a collaboration between the analyst and the patient. It can be very frightening if we also allow ourselves to be aware that we are all alone with, and dependent on, the patient. The patient may have outstanding athletic ability, and a manic state can lend great force to that ability. So a patient who is trying to prevent you from being helpful, creative or constructive sets you a considerable problem. How are you to continue to think clearly while someone is trying to murder you?

That is a comparatively simple situation, because you have the evidence of your senses and of the source from which the danger is arising. The position is more difficult when you are dealing with what we believe to be a mind, a spirit, a soul—or whatever the fashionable term is for it. I am sure that we all have experience of a great deal of education. So we are probably familiar with words like "spirit", "soul", "ego", "Buddha", "Brahma" and so on. Paradoxically what we may not be quite so familiar with is the name which would seem to us to be most suitable for the "thing" that we are dealing with when we are all alone with someone who comes to us for help. If the patient tries to throw you out of your window, it may be difficult to appreciate that he comes to you because he wants help. This same force which may be manifesting itself in a physical struggle with you, is what he has to live with. So he may be afraid that you will not be able to resist him physically and is terrified that he himself may not be able to resist or deal with that terrifying force.

In the practice of psychoanalysis—as opposed to the theory—your problem is, are you able to see such facts as are available? Some of them are easier than others: a physician can train his powers of observation so that he can see that the patient's countenance is not displaying a beautiful colouration of the cheeks such as would be appropriate to exercise or perfect health; he may be able to distinguish between the blush of rude health and something which he can say, if he understands the language spoken by the body, is the sign of an infection. The patient may be hostile to the mental helper, whether he is an analyst or whatever his position. What is the source of that hostility? Does it arise from within the individual, or is it an infection derived from the culture of which he is a member?

I have lived long enough to have had the experience of knowing that at one time psychoanalysis was all the rage amongst the intelligentsia. I am sure all of us can remember times when particular attitudes or beliefs were fashionable. I remember when it was fashionable to read *The Forsythe Saga* [John Galsworthy]; it was then forgotten; it was then revived, thanks to the dominance of television and the evidence of the eyes. So that story was rejuvenated—apparently. However—and this is a difficult point to describe—what really matters is the *real* Forsythe Saga, the fundamental story, the facts, reality. The only thing that I can call it is "the truth". That is not going to be affected by the fashion or by whatever we may happen to think about it.

Changing over to something more scientific like mathematics: the visual geometry of Euclid—lines, points, circles—proved gradually, in the course of a hundred years or so, to be inadequate to the human beings who used it. But I think that there was a *real* geometry which was also, as it were, trying to get expressed. Putting that in a different way: real geometry was implicit in Euclidean geometry. That truth, that *implicit* truth, was a kind of sleeping beauty waiting to be rescued, waiting for someone or something to break through the barriers of thorns and weeds and awaken the true geometry. In other words, Euclidean geometry and all its adherents had built up a barrier against the emergence of the truth, until at last the dominance of the eyes and the pictures of lines and circles was overthrown by the coordinate discovery and the application of algebraic thought to geometry. The truth hadn't altered; the truth that was implicit in Euclidean geometry became explicit.

This is one more example of the point that I have already made: an activity like psychoanalysis is fashionable, and fashions change. If, therefore, there is any truth in psychoanalysis or any truth in psychiatry, then it would be helpful if any of us could do anything to make that truth explicit. But it does mean cutting through an enormous growth of brambles, thorns, rationalizations. What we cannot afford to lose sight of is the main goal—the truth. Our own mental capacity has to be nourished, but there is nobody to choose for us; we have to be capable of respecting the truth whether that truth is expressed by our patients, our colleagues, our musicians, painters or religious authorities. So anyone who has respect for the truth deserves our support, and we have to deserve it. If we are to help our manic, depressive, schizophrenic or neurotic patient, we ourselves have to be worthy of respect. That can be partially dealt with by going to analysts and others who might help us to get to know who we really are. But in the position in which we find ourselves—a position which, it could be said, we have inherited— we *are* the authority, we *are* the parents, and there is no one for us to go to excepting ourselves. To modify that statement: while attempting to help a patient, as a sort of accidental fringe benefit we also learn something about ourselves.

To fall back again on the simple model of actual physical warfare: if, by any chance, we survive, we can learn something about ourselves. A book written in the First World War described a situation of perpetual and never-ceasing war—the war of the mind. The writer quoted the statement which was made long before psychoanalysis had even been thought of: "From that warfare there is no release". Here we can make breaks in this discussion, take rests, but that does not mean that the warfare takes a rest—it does not. Disease—mental disease, physical disease—does not take a holiday. That is why we have to be so robust, so healthy. Whatever our difficulties may be, we have to remember to be concerned not with our problems, but with the work in hand—the work which never stops whether we are there to do it or not. There was a famous warrior named Crylon to whom Henry IV said, "Go hand yourself, brave Crylon; we fought at Arc and you were not there."

Q: I have always felt that what we think about other people is bound to have some effect on them, even if we don't reveal our feelings.

Bion: That awareness could be regarded as part of the evidence for the existence of the human mind. It is usually fairly easy to see that you can be affected by a physical contact with someone or something which is not you. A child may bump into a table or chair, or hurt itself by falling down; it then wants to hit the table or chair or the floor because it has been naughty and has hurt it. The point is not quite so easy to see—if one can call it easy at all—when you are dealing with states of mind; that is when you are aware that you have come "in contact" with somebody who is not you. That "character" does not appear to be observable by what we have hitherto regarded as our physical senses—our sense of sight, of smell, of hearing and so on. Nevertheless, even an infant seems to be able to tell when it is all alone and also when the object on which it depends is present. In that respect the discovery and awareness of dependence, and the discovery and awareness of being all alone, are fundamental. Those fundamental feelings, thoughts and ideas can still be stirred many years later. Of course, it is obvious that we are dependent on the existence of something which is not us and, at the same time, that we are alone with the thing on which we are dependent. But as analysts we depend upon and we are alone with what we call "a mind". It is therefore important that we should not be overwhelmed by the latest fashion either of belief or disbelief, but should still remain capable of exercising such judgement as we have with regard to facts which are insensible.

At a time of turmoil, at a time when the leaders of the country were carrying out a revolution against the existing order, Milton wrote, "So much the rather thou, Celestial Light, / shine inward, and the mind through all her powers / Irradiate. . . ."

As analysts we have to make contact with somebody who comes to us for help. We are just as fallible, just as vulnerable, as any officer, NCO, or any one of their troops. As responsible people we do not have the privilege of being able to be ill, or to run away, or to be dominated by freely expressed emotions. We are just as much cowards as any of our troops; we are just as fallible as anybody that we are trying to help. In one way or another, we find ourselves inheriting a position of authority; how we have got there it might be very difficult to say. Even if you look back on the history of your own life, it will still be difficult to say how it comes about that you are in the position of being one of the authorities, one of the helpers. Victor Hugo described the experience which is shared by an army and its opponents as one of terror. We harbour the illusion that the enemy is very powerful, brave, well-trained, well-equipped: the enemy probably shares the same emotions about our own army. But if a poet is able to ignore these uniforms—mental and physical—then it is possible for him to see that the experience which is shared by both armies is one of terror.

This complicated situation was illustrated at Christmas time in 1914 when the opposing troops of the British and German armies fraternized and played football against each other in no-man's land on the day which was supposed to be the anniversary of the birth of Christ. To imitate Wellington: I don't know what effect that had on the enemy, but I can say that it terrified the Staff.

The further we get from the fighting line—the practice of psychoanalysis, mental health, psychiatry—the more we become aware of the ferocity of the staff, the ferocity of the theoreticians. If they had their way, the bloodshed would be terrible.

This seems to be what the speaker who asked this question was talking about. I am sorry to have given such a long-winded answer—the thing itself is much shorter: the real experience of affecting the patient and of being affected by the patient is almost instantaneous.

Q: I'd like to take up Dr Bion's earlier invitation to talk about difficulties we have met with in our work. Let me tell you about a patient who was diagnosed with a fatal disease—acute leukaemia—after two years of analysis. The patient was only partially informed. He dreamt that *he was on a couch or table, which was both the analyst's couch and the transfusion table; he was about to fall, but then seemed to be resting on a pivot, about which he was able to turn horizontally.* In this situation you can't say that the dream symbolizes time—the clock concept—but you have to say that the patient himself *is* time: he is clock time. If the patient is time and not the symbol of time, let me ask Dr Bion what the analyst must be, or can be.

BION: We can approach this problem, first of all, from a general standpoint and express a general principle. We conform to a certain discipline which we have acquired or been taught. However, as a practising doctor or analyst, you close down your view and concentrate your attention on an area which is more restricted. To put it in more philosophical terms, the general principle is being transformed into a particular instance.

If you were to ask me what my job is, I couldn't tell you, but I can tell you what *I* think it is. It is up to you to decide—you are the only person who can—what *you* think your job is. Narrowing this down further, let us look at this particular person of whom I have hearsay evidence which I have been told by the last speaker. This patient's death doesn't interest me any more than his birth. That tiny little bit between birth and death—that *does* interest me. It may be a very small space indeed, because there is such a thing as infant mortality, death at birth—or death at death. So I don't think there is a great deal in this tiny little space between the moment of being born and the termination of that life—as I say, it can terminate virtually at the start, or even before the person ever becomes "conscious", as we call it.

This particular patient is said to be dying. That again doesn't impress me; we are all dying since we are, in fact, living. But it does interest me if the life and the space which is left is worth living or not. We do not know what we shall die of—I am sure that some-body sooner or later will oblige by diagnosing it. In this instance, it is said to be lymphatic leukaemia. It might be something else; it might be the death of the person's mind. I have come across people whose bodies still survive, but as far as their minds, spirits or souls are concerned they are dead. To turn again to this more particular view, this very small view in which we don't bother very much about all these general principles, then we need to focus on the question, is there any spark which could be fanned into a flame so that the person could live whatever life, whatever capital, he still has in the bank? How much *vital* capital has this person? And could he be assisted to use that capital to good effect?

Although this patient is said to have leukaemia, a fatal com-plaint, since I cannot foretell the future I don't know what he will die of; I *do* know that it won't be death, because death is not a disease. That is simply one of these impressive caesuras.

This patient is living in a certain culture—I gather that he hasn't been told that he has lymphatic leukaemia, and I doubt that it would mean much to him anyway, if he is a layman. but I have no reason to doubt that he can interpret certain physical facts. What is his interpretation of the sort of behaviour to which he is subjected by his culture? Who does he think the analyst is? Is he somebody to help him to live, or to die? Most of us—to widen the view again—

can be relied upon to indulge in plenty of activities which are much more likely to kill us than to make us live; we take things into our alimentary systems which are poisonous. There is nothing wrong with alcohol, but we can use it for purposes of poisoning our physical system; there is nothing wrong with taking air into our lungs, but we can indeed breathe polluted air or smoke and inhale the fumes. In Britain there is a warning compulsorily printed on all packets of cigarettes and on all advertisements for tobacco: "Smoking is injurious to health." That statement, that warning, has become part of the ritual of smoking; it is part of the beautiful, seductive picture of the pleasures and delights of smoking. It is made respectable and even scientific by saying "Low Tar". I have never smoked tar in my life—I am not interested in buying tar, so I can see how virtuous I am because I don't smoke tar. Now, I can get on with smoking tobacco—unless, of course, the manufacturers should feel it was more profitable to sell me low tar. I can see that it might be cheaper to make a big cigarette with a large wad of cotton instead of the rather more expensive tobacco leaf.

Narrow down the view again to get nearer to what we are concerned with: a mind. While the body of this patient is dependent on various sorts of somatic nourishment, what are we to provide him with by way of mental nourishment? By this time the analyst certainly knows a lot about the patient, so he could tell the patient all sorts of things about lymphatic leukaemia. To widen the picture, I could say, "In my opinion he should tell him the truth." Narrow it again: what is the truth? What does the analyst know about it, and what could the patient understand if the analyst tried to communicate with him?

I am sorry to take such a long time to discuss such very simple points. We still haven't got to the point—namely, what the analyst is to say that this patient could understand. It is possible that the patient could feel that this particular helper is more interested in his living a life worth living than in the various rituals and procedures which are appropriate to dying. If that is the case, he could feel that this object with which he gets into contact—even if it isn't a physical contact—might be friendly and helpful. That may or may not be psychoanalysis—I am not bothering with that because I am not interested at this point in theory but in practice, in life. Whether the patient is at the beginning of his life, at birth, or whether he is at the other end of the spectrum, at death, he can feel the presence of a friendly or health-giving object.

I think it is very difficult to resolve to avoid the truth and to start telling some sort of agreeable lie. It is hard work, it doesn't seem to me to be worth doing, and, as a result, one's own mind, character, personality is polluted. Our capacity to speak the truth dies through the lies we tell other people.

Let us try to bring to bear on this problem the combined wisdom of all of us. If you were in this position, what would you say to the patient? Apparently he had what he calls "a dream". That means that he was in a different state of mind from that in which he is when he is wide awake, "conscious", and carrying on a conversation with you. The dream he tells you is, in fact, what he, in the state of mind in which he is when conscious, thinks happened when he was asleep. In this conversation, what should we be most impressed by? The fact that he is awake and conscious? Or that he is also in the state of mind which is a "hangover" from the state of mind in which he is asleep?

In the quotation I mentioned from Milton's *Paradise Lost*, he says, ". . . there plant eyes, all mist from thence / Purge and disperse . . .". Can the analyst forget all that he has heard or learnt about lymphatic leukaemia? These "facts" form a mist, obscuring the truth which might help this person to live his remaining hours, weeks, months, years perhaps, in a way that is worth living.

It might be possible to draw the patient's attention to the fact that he fears that when he is off his guard—as he is when he is asleep—then the analyst may subject him to the same sort of treatment as all the other doctors. So that what is in fact only a psychoanalytic conversation would appear to be something which was sucking the vital substance out of him. His blood may be very defective stuff—it has a lot of white cells which are not beneficially operative—but it is the only blood he has.

Translating that into mental terms: the patient is well aware of the defects of his character. But he does not want to lose such soul as he has. You could try saying, "You are afraid that I am trying to cure you, but that my cure is going to kill you by taking away anything good that you have." I don't want to attach any importance to that particular interpretation, because, in fact, it is worthless—*I* am not treating this patient and therefore I don't know.

There is no outrage that I know of which is greater than the one you permit when you allow someone not yourself into the privacy of your own mind. So the patient can be frightened of the analyst, and frightened of himself for talking to an analyst. The analyst will certainly be subjected to pressures; he is liable to be attacked— "Why tease a dying man with all this stuff which might be appropriate *if* the patient was going to live?" It is difficult to defend your position, which would mean saying something like, "Yes, but this patient has still got a few minutes, hours, days, weeks left to live, and that is why it would be helpful for him to know what I am telling him." Whether we are in good health or whether we are suffering from a fatal disease, it may still be worth while to know how to use our minds.

Q: And the survivors? What do you have to say about the survivors?

BION: The survivors, of course, are able to go on thinking and feeling. The fact of death is so impressive that it nearly always stirs up a turmoil; thoughts and feelings which we have forgotten become conscious. In that way we have an experience which is more powerful than any psychoanalytic experience because it is real life. In an organized, socialized group, the death of an important person—or the death of a symbol of an important person, somebody who might represent or remind you of a father or mother of a nation—is dealt with by elaborate rituals. Sometimes they involve the participation of the armed forces, who make a slow march behind the body to the place of burial to the accompaniment of pieces of music like the "Dead March" from *Saul* [Handel oratorio], or, "The Flowers of the Forest Are All Gone Away" [traditional: commemorates those killed in the Battle of Flodden in Scotland in 1513]. As soon as the body has been disposed of, the troops, representing the nation, march off in quick time. The slow march is the depression, mourning up to the moment of burial, and then—quick march! That, I think, is a profound group reaction: it is a reminder that when the dead are dead, that is the end of the story; it is time to get on with living.

I think we might also consider the reciprocal of this—should we interfere with anybody who *wants* to die? Does the fact that we purport to be helpers entitle us to interfere at all with somebody who does not want to be helped? There is a difficulty here: we have to consider what evidence leads us to suppose that the individual does not wish to be interfered with or to pay any attention whatever to such warnings, opinions or advice as may be conducive to longevity. It matters very much, of course, whether the person who does not want to live would pollute the atmosphere for the survivors.

Who or what are the forces which are liable to be conducive to *mental* death? It would be useful to know what is good mental nourishment—which would imply also knowing what is bad. The advantage of a group situation is that you can survey the entire group and possibly detect sources of infection in it. The entire group could remind you of various aspects of your own personality at different stages in your development. Instead of seeing it in narrative form, from A to Z, you could, so to speak, see all the letters of the alphabet spread out on one plane. That is a pictorial way of getting rid of the time component—we exchange a temporal component for a visual emphasis of the spatial component. Here and there you can see for yourself the sort of behaviour, activity, which has been designed to destroy the group's capacity for learning or developing its own abilities. When you feel the need for silence, and possibly the chance of hearing your own thoughts or ideas, the silence can be destroyed. The noise becomes so great that you cannot hear yourself think, This is one of your problems if you are concerned with education: with trying to make available, to people who don't know, such experience or knowledge as you have. Parents find themselves in the same position *vis-à-vis* their children—they would like to do something for them. And it also applies to the human family, not simply blood relations.

Q: I have on occasion given some attention to what you might call a state of slight chronic depersonalization—that is, a state in which mental capacity is diminished both in waking life and in sleep, so that the possibility of experiencing facts or emotions, or even sense data, is reduced. It seems to me that such a situation has components that stem from the group and from the individual. Can Dr Bion tell us how we might define or find coordinates to locate the source of such a mental state, and why—at least in my own experience—emerging from such a situation, even if it is acknowledged to be useful and growth-promoting, proves to be painful, dangerous and tiring.

BION: As usual, it is easier to talk about it in its more exaggerated forms: a patient who never seems to mention himself at all—I am thinking of a particular patient—but constantly pours out information about the characteristics of a very great number of people, all members of the society of which he finds himself a member. Such a state as that could be a later stage in what Melanie Klein described as an omnipotent phantasy of infancy, the phantasy of getting rid of the character or personality. The grown person sees faults everywhere: that seems to me to be not dissimilar from this theory of evacuating all the characteristics which are feared and disliked, and then being persecuted by them from outside. Every analytic interpretation, every person and thing, comes over as a persecution because they remind the patient of himself and his fear of these selves which become reunited in his own personality.

Let us get back to this *chronic* case. Could we again fall back on the group situation and say that between the lot of us we represent a *chronic* state? We are not only individuals to whom we attach some importance because of our individual view of ourselves *as* individuals, but we are individual bits out of a total pattern. What I want to know more about is what is meant by this word "chronic". Is it, in fact, a reference to "chronos", to time? What is this "chronic" or "chronos" about? What is the meaning of it?

Q: I think I can be more precise: it seems to me that "chronic" describes a state where there is no clearly definable distinction between two situations. Second, it seems to me that "chronic" also has the property of not being easily distinguishable, in the sense of not manifesting itself as an obvious fact.

BION: This may be the sort of thing that psychoanalysts are trying to describe when they talk about a "latency period". I find it easier to believe that what we have just had described to us is a latency *state* rather than a latency *period*. In this way, the patient can at any time present a somewhat featureless landscape. Is there anything which sticks up above the level of uniformity? One thing, of course, occurs to me at once—namely, the presenting quality of nullity. I will try to put it pictorially by reminding you of the termination of the fifth book of the *Aeneid* by Virgil: he describes Palinurus, who was the helmsman of the ship which is to give directions to the entire fleet. Somnus presents himself to Palinurus and puts forward the seductive view that all is going well. The sea is calm, there are no clouds, there is no danger anywhere. Palinurus, however, says that he is not so innocent as to be taken in by the calm face presented by the Mediterranean Sea. He ties himself to the tiller and to the stern sheets, but the god hurls him into the sea with such force that he is drowned and carries with him the stern of the ship. Now look at the calm and uniform surface presented by this patient—there are no features. What has happened to the storm?

What is to be said to this patient? There must be something which causes his musculature to react and to bring him into the analyst's view. We could point out to him that there seems to be absolutely no reason whatever for coming to talk to an analyst. The only thing wrong with this story is the patient's presence. So we could try to draw attention to the fact that there is a mystery which confronts the pair of you, and that is the mystery of a fact.

If you draw the patient's attention to this fact, then he may be able to contribute something further; he may not know much about himself, but what he does know is a great deal more than anybody else is ever likely to know. The patient knows—nobody else can— what it is like to be him and to have his thoughts and feelings. So if you can draw attention to this mystery that he is in the room, then he may be able, from his vast store of knowledge—it *is* vast, even if the patient is a child—to throw some further light. And then it may be possible for you to give another interpretation.

Take the previous patient we heard about: if he is able to interpret all these peculiar facts about a hospital ward, a bed, hypodermic needles and so on, what does he think they mean? What does *he* think is the interpretation of all that apparatus? Why talk to the analyst?

One could say that the question is the same in both these cases: why talk to the analyst? Of course, it could be because the patient is sure that the analyst knows nothing about him and will not say anything frightening or disturbing. But that is very unlikely, because most of us have in our time been told stories of one kind and another with the express purpose of terrifying us. We even play games like soldiers at war. But what is the game they want to play with the analyst now? Why do these two people talk to the analyst? What is it a part of? What is this conversational intercourse about? I borrow a term from the sexual experience because I think that there is something in the capacity to converse which is not altogether unlike the capacity to have a physical relationship. The psychoanalytic conversation is a kind of childhood game, just as a childhood game is a kind of implicit reality; it is referable to something in the present. This group meeting is referable to something we don't know about—namely, the future. Are there some vestigial remains in both these conversations? Is there something which reminds you of the wreckage, the vestiges of a previous conversation? Are there any vestiges, any discernible bits, of wreckage which remind you of love or hate?

Here we can assume that there must be some reason for wanting to meet together. That doesn't mean to say that our feelings of dislike or hatred have disappeared, any more than the storms have disappeared for ever because the surface of the Mediterranean is calm. So even as we survey the dominance of the friendly relationship which causes us all to come together, what about the vestiges of the *rest* of our personalities? If we want to break up the meeting or destroy the furniture, what has happened to those impulses? Could it be faintly reminiscent of civilization itself? There is a thin film of civilization which covers all our human community. The United States, the United Kingdom, and now the United Nations—how united we all are . . .

FRANCESCO CORRAO: The group is probably a place—*locus* or *topos*—a privileged place where space and time, feminine and masculine, hate and love, truth and falsehood, all come together. Now, this coming-together is violent, hard to bear and hard to transform. So we need the support and guidance of a way of thinking and a method that is problematic and unifying at one and the same time. My feeling is that Dr Bion has supplied us—is supplying us—with this way of thinking and that he himself represents a strength in the here-and-now, because he embodies the strength of thought—its function, its use and its communication. These group research centres—the first, the Pollaiolo, and then the others—concentrate on an area defined by the relationship between the group and the analytic function.

After all, it is worth remembering that the Bionian view is generated by an extremely intensified and amplified analytic experience. My feeling—or perhaps I should say, our feeling—is of deep gratitude to Dr Bion, for having enabled us to partake of the depth of his thought.

BION: I thank you very much for that expression of gratitude. I hope it doesn't appear to be ungracious if I say that I can compare your description of my contributions with the fact of which I am aware and which I don't very much like. The nearest image I can give to it is this: like a leaf falling off a tree—one never knows which side up it will land. And when I look back on what I know about my life, I would never have been able to guess that I would be here today, at this time and in such a position.

There is a passage in a poem by Yeats, *Solomon and the Witch*, in which he talks about "Choice and Chance":

And when at last that murder's over
Maybe the bride-bed brings despair,
For each an imagined image brings
And finds a real image there;

[W. B. Yeats, *Solomon and the Witch*]

"Journeys end in lovers meeting / Every wise man's son doth know" [Shakespeare, *Twelfth Night*]. I don't think they end in lovers meeting; they *start* at that point. Is there any vestige, do you think, in this hospital bed and the analyst's couch, any remains of the possibility of a loving or positive relationship between this person who calls himself an analyst and this other person who call himself something else? What is this group likely to give birth to? What thought or idea or action? And what relationship is likely to occur between it and some other group? Love or hate? Fight or flight? Dependence or freedom?

INDEX

Abraham, K., 28, 29
absolute space, 33
adolescence, caesura of, 80
algebraic geometry, 54
alpha-elements, 12
amnesia, 36
analysis, dyadic situation of, 65
ancestors, our indebtedness to, 23, 29
Andersen, H. C., "The Nightingale", 81
antivivisectionism, 80
"arbitrium", 83
art:
    communication through, 49
    truth in, 43
articulate language, 19, 82
articulate speech, 5, 12, 20, 22, 41, 48–49, 59, 64

Baghavad Gita, 62, 85
beta-elements, 12
binaural hearing, 70
binocular vision, 70
birth:
    as birthday, 8
    caesura of, 2, 25, 53, 79, 80
        impressive, 45, 64
    initiation of, by infant, 60
    trauma of, 2, 8, 25
    repetition of, in analysis, 8
borderline psychotic patients, 7, 41, 42, 52, 60, 65
Brahms, J., 74

branchial clefts, 3
British Institute of Psycho-Analysis, 1
Brower, A., 14
Buddha, 84, 91

caesura(s), 11, 12, 25, 53, 80, 87, 96
    of birth, 2, 25
    "impressive", 2, 45
Cartesian coordinates, 33, 44, 54, 86
claustrophobic space, 15
Clough, A., 31
coherence, 83
communicability, limits of, 40
communication:
    through art, 6
    articulate, 53
    non-linguistic, 7
    nonverbal, 6, 7, 8, 19, 37
    patient's lack of ability for, 20
    pictorial, 6, 24, 81
    primitive, 21
    verbal, 5, 9, 62, 83
    see also language; speech
conjugate complex, 31
Corrao, F., 103
countertransference, 27–32, 64
Crylon, 93
"cure", 24, 42, 87
curiosity, 32, 71

dangerous adventure, analysis as, 24, 41, 89–93
daydreams, 48

suicide, 52, 90
superego, 68, 83
supersoul, 68
symbols, intrapsychic, 6

Tacitus, 84
thinking/thought(s), 8, 10, 65, 74,
        75, 85
    group, 56
    mathematical, 11, 14
    tools for, analyst's invention of,
        73–74
    wild: *see* wild thought(s)
    -without-a-thinker, 47, 63–65
time, 33, 37, 53, 95, 100, 101, 103
    concept of, 69–71
Tolstoy, L., *War and Peace*, 8
touch, sense of, 2
transference, 27, 28, 29, 32, 64
    manifestation, 28
    relationship, 68
truth, 81, 88, 92–93, 97–98, 103
    in analytic communication, 48
    in artistic communication, 43
    problem of, 72–74
    see also interpretations, truth

unconscious, the, language of, 35
Upanishads, 85

Valerian, 55
Valéry, P., 37
Virgil, 25, 53
    Aeneid, 102
vocabulary, analyst's, precision of,
        importance of, 5

war of mind, 93
Wellington, Duke of, 90, 95
wild thought(s), 44, 47–49, 59, 61,
        65, 76
Winnicott, D. W., 60
wisdom, 57, 65–66, 77, 98
    vs. intelligence, 53, 55, 59
    tree of, 32
Wordsworth, W., "Lines Composed
        a Few Miles Above Tintern
        Abbey", 74
writing, 67
    communication via, 67

Yeats, W. B., *Solomon and the Witch,*
        104